AMERICA IN WAX

An armchair tour visiting the famous people and fascinating events, from the earliest explorers to the present as captured in wax museums throughout the United States, Canada, and abroad

by GENE GURNEY

CROWN PUBLISHERS, INC. New York

Also by the Author

THE UNITED STATES COAST GUARD: A PICTORIAL HISTORY
BEAUTIFUL WASHINGTON, D.C.
A PICTORIAL HISTORY OF THE UNITED STATES ARMY
THE WAR IN THE AIR
HOW TO SAVE YOUR LIFE ON THE
NATION'S HIGHWAYS AND BYWAYS
THE AIR FORCE MUSEUM

All of the museums mentioned in the captions accompanying the illustrations are listed in the Directory of Wax Museums at the end of this book, with addresses, road directions, telephone numbers, and hours. Illustrations not credited to a museum were photographed by the author.

Printed in the United States of America
Published simultaneously in Canada by General Publishing Company Limited

Designed by Laurie Zuckerman and Rhea Braunstein

LIBRARY OF CONGRESS CATALOGING IN PUBLICATION DATA

Gurney, Gene.
America in wax.

Includes index.
1. Waxworks. 2. United States—History—Miscellanea. I. Title.
GV1836.G87 1976 973'.074 76-43972
ISBN 0-517-52524-0

CONTENTS

1 AN ANCIENT ART

Wax sculpture ranks as one of the more ancient of the art forms that have fascinated the human race over the centuries. The art of fashioning shapes in wax is so old that its origins are uncertain. But it is known that beekeeping was practiced by many ancient civilizations and beeswax was used for modeling in addition to its use as a preservative. The pale yellow substance can be shaped easily; it melts at low heat for casting and it mixes well with coloring materials.

The Egyptians used wax in the embalming process and they created wax figures of deities which played a role in funeral rites. The practice of making a wax figure of an enemy, the oldest known form of sorcery, may have begun with the Egyptians who were also skilled in modeling fruits in wax.

In ancient Greece wax images of the gods had an honored place in religious ceremonies. The Greeks excelled in using beeswax to make lifelike dolls for children. The fact that the court of Alexander the Great is reported to have included a wax sculptor gives some indication of the popularity of wax figures among these peoples.

Patrician families of ancient Rome carefully preserved wax masks of their ancestors, which were brought forth on ceremonial occasions and carried in funeral processions. During the final days of the Saturnalia festival, which celebrated the winter solstice, Romans gave one another presents of wax models of fruit and small statues made of wax.

From Rome the practice of wax modeling spread northward. In medieval Europe and later, the faithful presented religious figures of wax to the churches; and the superstitious thrust long pins into wax images of hated persons in the belief that the man or woman represented would somehow be injured.

In many countries wax sculptors customarily made masks of the faces of monarchs and other personages. In Britain the practice can be traced to the fourteenth century. In some cases the entire figure was modeled in wax or a combination of wax, wood, and plaster. At the funeral of a great man his elab-

LEFT: Westminster Abbey's wax effigy of Charles II is seen here in the clothing worn under the monarch's Garter robes. The face is said to be a remarkable likeness of the British king who reigned from 1660 until 1685.

CENTER: Although Lord Nelson, the English admiral who defeated the French at Trafalgar, was buried in London's St. Paul's Cathedral when he died in 1805, this effigy of the popular hero was installed in Westminster Abbey in an attempt to attract larger audiences.

RIGHT: The wax likeness of Madame Tussaud seen here was modeled by Madame herself when she was eighty-one. The self-portrait is on display at Madame Tussaud's in London.

orately dressed wax effigy was carried to the grave. After the burial, the effigy was installed in the church where friends of the deceased could leave poems praising him. Westminster Abbey in London still retains and displays wax representations of King Charles II, William Pitt, Lord Nelson, and several other dignitaries.

Early bronze and metalwork was almost always cast from wax models. The process, known as cire perdue (lost wax), involved modeling in wax the head, figure, or other form that the artist wished to cast in metal. The carved wax surface was covered with clay and allowed to harden. The next step involved heating the mold to melt the wax which was removed through a vent and replaced with molten metal. After the metal had set, the clay mold was broken, leaving the artist with his finished work. The great early masters used this method.

Exhibitions of wax sculpture, or waxworks, became popular in Europe during the eighteenth century. In his *London Journal* Boswell describes a visit in 1763 to the waxworks of a Mrs. Salmon. "It is excellent in its kind and amused me very well for a quarter of an hour," he wrote.

The most famous waxworks of them all, Madame Tussaud's, had its beginning in Bern, Switzerland, where a Doctor Curtius made wax models of human limbs and organs as substitutes for cadavers, which were almost impossible to obtain. A talented modeler, Curtius extended his efforts to miniature wax portraits, which attracted much favorable attention, including that of a cousin of Louis XV of France.

By 1770 Dr. Curtius had moved to Paris and opened a successful exhibition of life-sized portraits of notables of the day. A few years later his niece, Marie Grosholtz, the future Madame Tussaud, became his apprentice.

A talented modeler like her uncle, Marie made a portrait of the aged Voltaire when she was seventeen. The waxwork still survives. Soon the young artist was giving instructions in wax modeling to the royal court at Versailles,

LEFT: At the Hollywood Wax Museum the future Madame Tussaud appears as a young girl.

RIGHT: Madame Tussaud's storeroom at Wookey Hole in southwest England holds scores of heads that have been replaced by new ones at the London museum. Most of the heads eventually will be melted down and the wax used again. Some of the eyes will be reused, but hair has too short a life to be worth replanting. *Courtesy Madame Tussaud's*

but her teaching career was cut short by the advent of the French Revolution. After a short imprisonment on the suspicion that she was a Royalist, Marie was released when the revolutionaries decided to put her skill as a wax sculptor to use. She made death masks of some of the famous heads severed by the guillotine.

Following the Revolution, Marie Grosholtz turned to the modeling of less gory subjects, including Napoleon. She inherited her uncle's waxworks, which she ran with François Tussaud, whom she married in 1795. In 1802, however, she left Paris for England, taking seventy wax exhibits with her, and for the next thirty-three years she toured the United Kingdom with the popular Exhibition. In 1835, when she was seventy-four, Madame Tussaud acquired a permanent home for her waxworks in London's Baker Street. The present Madame Tussaud's is located not far away in Marylebone Road.

In spite of the popularity of Madame Tussaud's and other European waxworks, there was no permanent wax museum in the United States until 1949 when George L. Potter opened Potter's Wax Museum in St. Augustine, Florida. Other museums followed until today there are more than forty which attract several million Americans each year. There are ten or more in Canada just as popular.

Like their European counterparts, American wax museums stress personages of historical interest, although popular figures are well represented. In addition, many American museums pose wax figures in dioramas that re-create historical highlights of the area in which the museum is located.

The art of producing a wax likeness of a figure of historical or popular interest has changed little since Madame Tussaud's time. She probably made her earlier figures by forming a plaster mold directly on the head of her subject. But this method often produced a poor likeness if the weight of the plaster distorted the face, or the subject moved his facial muscles. To avoid these problems, wax sculptors began to model a likeness of their subject in clay. They

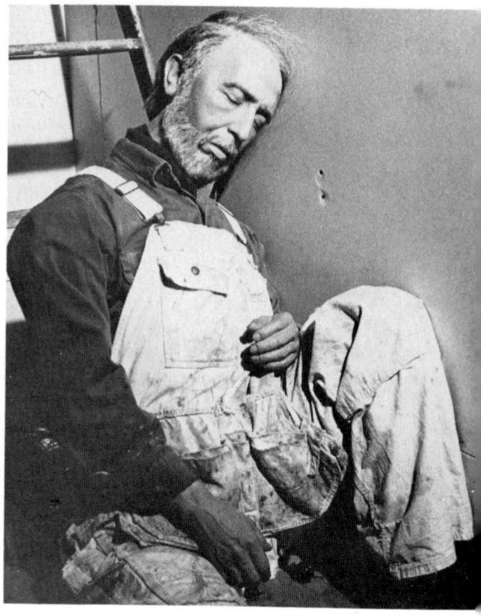

LEFT: In the lobby at Madame Tussaud's a wax bootblack appears to be shining the shoes of another wax figure.

RIGHT: This "workman" is a "breathing" self-portrait of Baltimore exhibits designer and sculptor Earl Dorfman who created figures for this Annapolis museum. Instead of wax, Dorfman's Wax Museum Enterprises uses polyvinyl chloride plastisol, a mixture of vinyl resins and plasticizers, the latter added for flexibility and softness. *Courtesy Annapolis Naval Historical Wax Museum*

then made a plaster mold from the clay model, the procedure that is still followed today.

During his preparations for creating an effigy, the sculptor carefully researches his subject. If possible, he spends some time with the subject making sketches and taking photographs and measurements. If that can't be done, the sculptor studies written descriptions, photographs, and portraits.

After carefully modeling the head of his subject in clay, the sculptor forms a plaster mold. Because it will be removed after hardening, the mold is made in several sections. Washed, dried and fitted back together, the mold is ready to receive the molten, tinted wax, or other substance, that will be poured into it. Most sculptors continue to use beeswax which, although very expensive, gives the appearance of human skin. There are some sculptors, however, who prefer to work with vinyl resins to which plasticizers have been added.

When a one-half-inch-or-more layer of wax next to the plaster mold has cooled and hardened, the remaining wax is poured out. The sculptor now has a hollow wax head that exactly duplicates the clay mold he made earlier.

At this stage a wax head is a yellowish pink in color, without hair, eyes, or teeth. Human hair as exactly matched as possible in color and texture to that of the subject is implanted with a needle, strand by strand, in the slightly warmed wax of the scalp. Eyes are also exactly matched to those of the subject. They are medical glass eyes, inserted from the inside of the hollow head and painstakingly set to focus at the right distance. Teeth are similar to human dentures. Skin coloring is applied with a brush, with due allowances for blemishes.

Although the head of a subject receives the most attention from the sculptor, he will mold the entire body in clay. Separate plaster casts are made for the head and the body, however. The parts of the body that will be covered by clothing are usually cast in polyester resin, but papier-mâché sometimes is used for the body parts that will be hidden. All exposed parts, such as the subject's

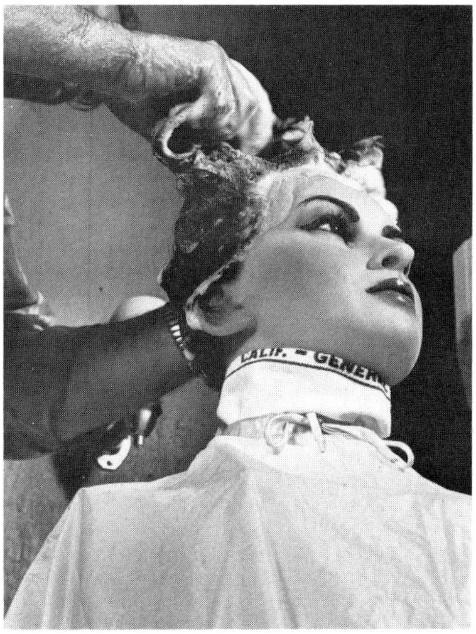

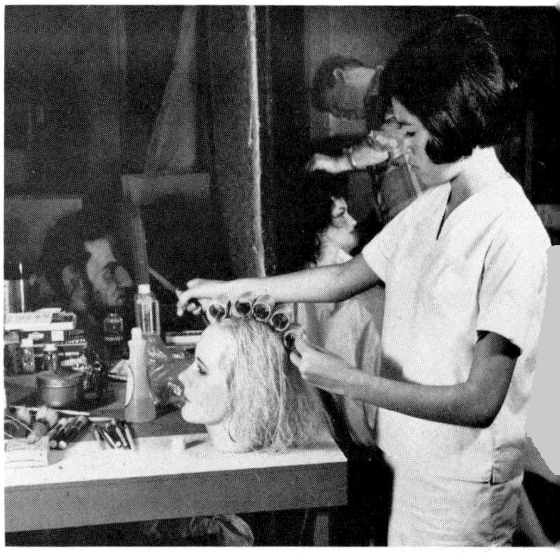

TOP: To preserve its lifelike appearance, a wax figure must undergo regular refurbishing. These photos, taken behind scenes at the Wax Museum at Fisherman's Wharf, show *(from left)* Abraham Lincoln getting his eyes cleaned, a shampoo in progress, and a hairdresser setting a wax model's hair. *Courtesy Wax Museum at Fisherman's Wharf*

CENTER, LEFT: A wax likeness of actor Steve McQueen receives a last-minute touch-up from a museum employee before going on display. *Courtesy Wax Museum at Fisherman's Wharf* RIGHT: A hair stylist works on singer Glen Campbell's hair. On Campbell's right is a likeness of Carol Burnett. *Courtesy Southwestern Historical Wax Museum*

LEFT: Lifelike wax figures man lobby desks such as at the London Wax Museum of Boston.

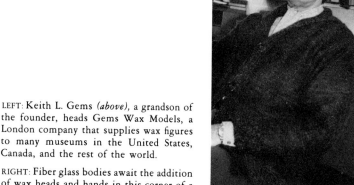

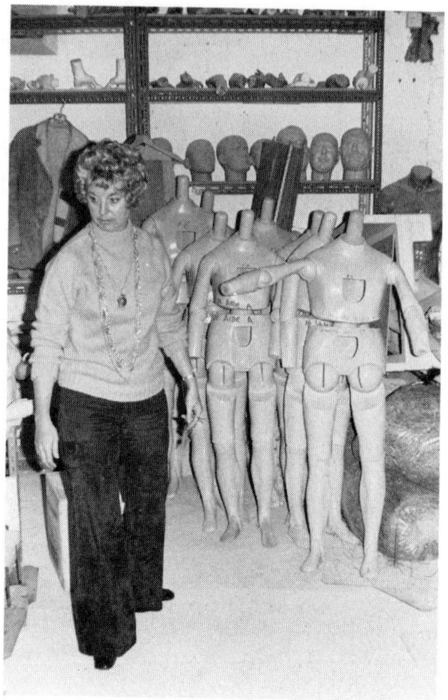

LEFT: Keith L. Gems *(above)*, a grandson of the founder, heads Gems Wax Models, a London company that supplies wax figures to many museums in the United States, Canada, and the rest of the world.

RIGHT: Fiber glass bodies await the addition of wax heads and hands in this corner of a Gems workroom. An employee stands at left.

hands, are cast in wax and carefully colored to correspond to the original. In some cases exposed parts, usually hands, are cast from life.

In selecting clothing for a wax subject, the emphasis is on authenticity and correctness of detail. In the case of living subjects, clothing and accessories may come from the subject's own wardrobe. Talented designers create other costumes after studying a subject's life and times. Care is taken to give the clothing the appearance it would have if it actually had been worn by the subject.

Madame Tussaud's makes all of the figures displayed in its London museum as well as for a second Madame Tussaud's in Amsterdam. Other museums acquire their figures from a number of sources. Gems Wax Models of London supplies many museums in the United States and Canada, although several United States firms make figures. Skilled artisans also work in Paris, Hong Kong, and Mexico City, among other places.

By presenting accurate, three-dimensional likenesses of men and women who have helped shape America's past, wax museums make history come alive for millions of visitors each year. In the exhibit halls of a wax museum famous men and women appear as they did at the height of their careers. They are dressed as they would have dressed at the time and they often are posed in a tableau re-creating an important event in which they played a part. Columbus comes ashore at San Salvador; Thomas Jefferson works on a draft of the Declaration of Independence; General George Washington prays for his men at Valley Forge; General Ulysses S. Grant accepts General Robert E. Lee's surrender at Appomattox. The exhibits cover the entire span of American history, from the discovery and exploration of a new continent to the manned landings on the moon. Through these vivid re-creations, Americans can relive the exciting events that made their country great.

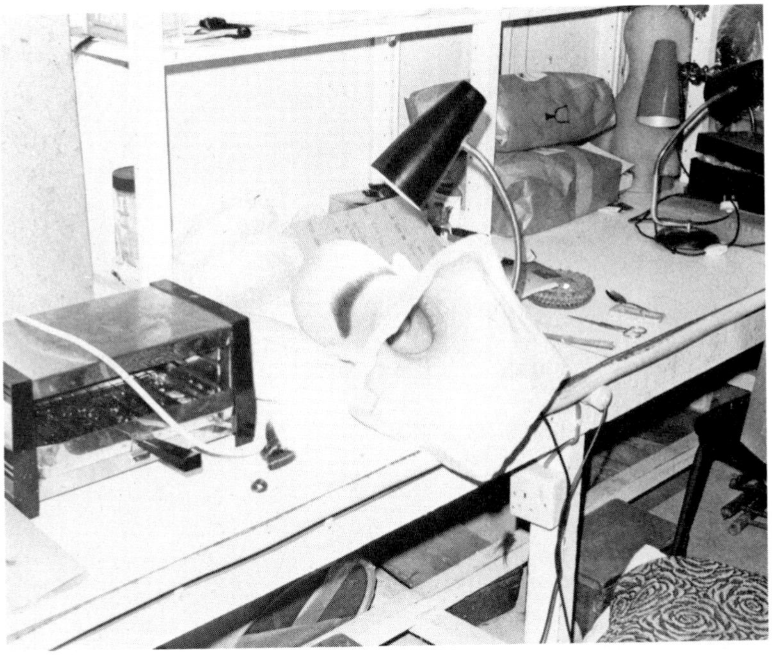

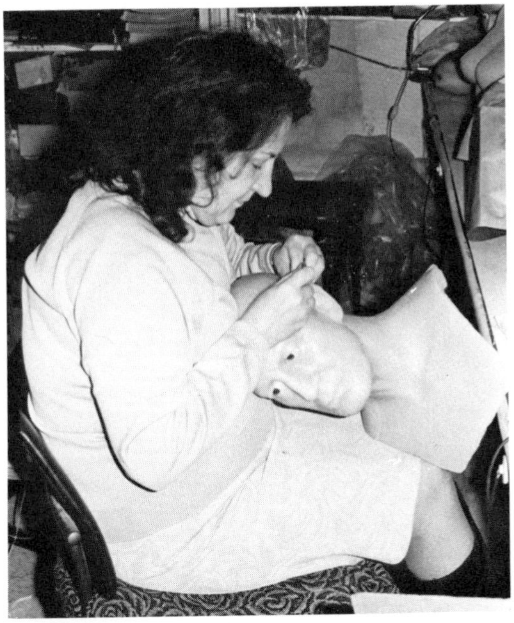

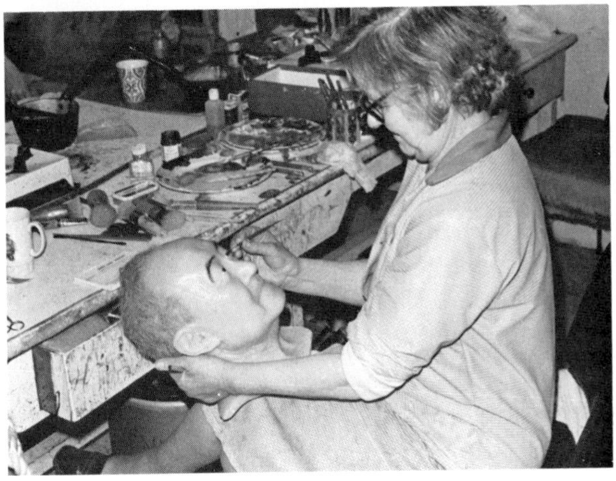

TOP, LEFT: The heater in the foreground holds a pan of beeswax which has been warmed to 87 degrees centigrade (172.4 F.), the temperature at which Gems artisans pour it into molds. A secret chemical compound has been added to the wax to help it to harden and to increase its resistance to extremes of heat and cold. RIGHT: Heat from a lamp warms the wax head on the worktable *(center)* prior to the insertion of hair.

CENTER, LEFT: Here, Vicki Piango, a Gems employe, uses a fine needle to painstakingly insert strands of human hair into a wax head.

RIGHT: Veteran Gems employe (of more than fifty years) and manager of the wax department Mrs. Wynne Mills *(center)* provides a wax head with a mustache.

LEFT: Here, the eyebrows of a wax head receive expert attention from one of Gems's skilled artisans.

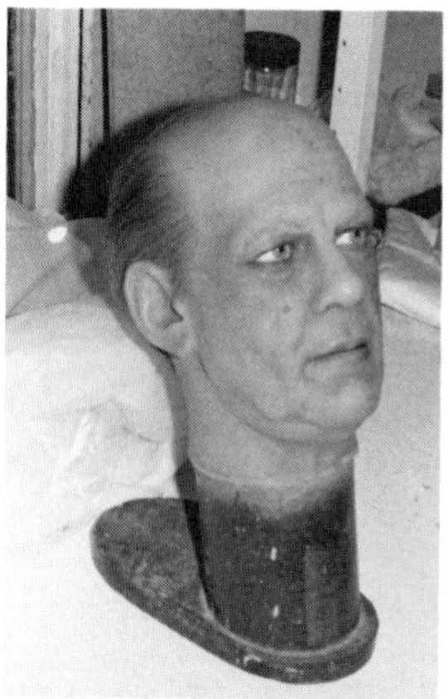

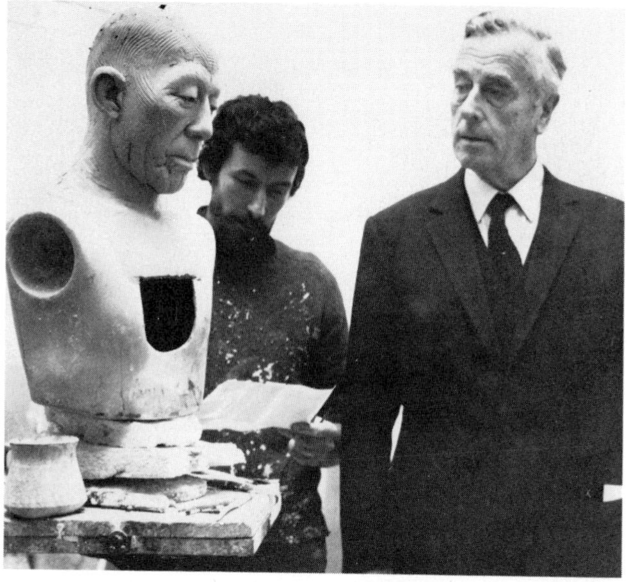

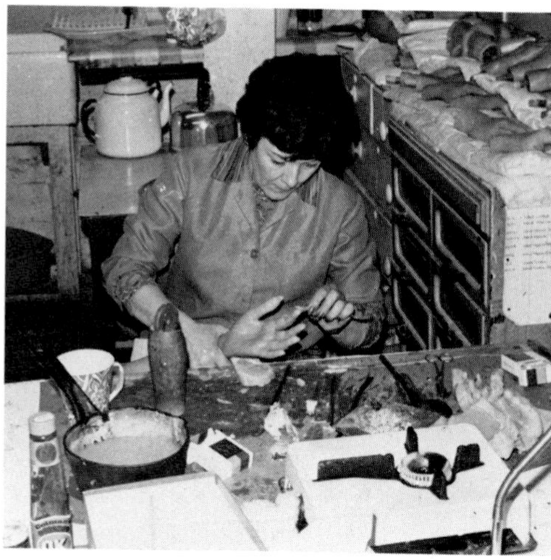

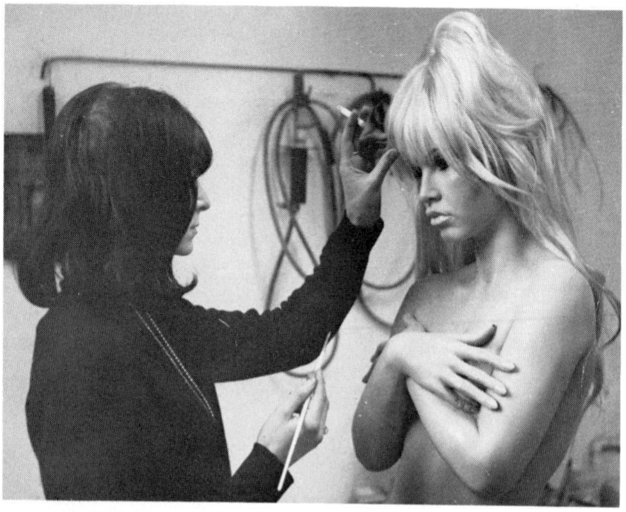

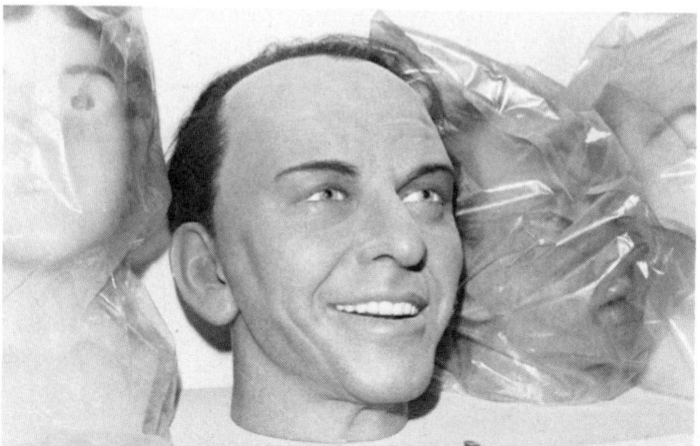

TOP LEFT: Two weeks after Gerald R. Ford became president of the United States, Gems Wax Models was ready to ship wax representations of him to its museum customers. The company prepares wax heads of all United States vice-presidents, "just in case." Here, a Ford head stands on a Gems worktable. CENTER: This photo was taken during a visit by Mountbatten to the Gems Wax Models workrooms. He is inspecting the clay head of his World War II opponent in Southeast Asia, Japanese General Susheiro Itagaki. *Courtesy Gems Wax Models* RIGHT: Fingernails receive as much care as any other part of a wax figure. Here, a Gems artisan manicures the nails of a wax hand.

SECOND ROW, LEFT: A Gems artist uses a brush and wax paint to give the correct skin tone to a nearly completed figure of French actress Brigitte Bardot. *Courtesy Gems Wax Models* CENTER: Bardot shares the Gems workroom with a head *(on right)* that will become part of a Sigmund Freud figure. *Courtesy Gems Wax Models.* RIGHT: A likeness of Catherine Howard, the fifth wife of Henry VIII, will wear this jeweled headdress.

THIRD ROW: The authentic Continental Army officer's uniform seen here awaits the completion of a representation of George Washington ordered by one of Gem's American customers.

BOTTOM: Gems keeps a supply of finished heads on hand to fill rush orders for popular wax figures. Seen here is a Frank Sinatra head.

TOP: Seen here, the National Historical Wax Museum's Dorfman-designed Salem witchcraft trials set with museum owner Frank Dennis *(second from right)* standing next to the figure of the Puritan judge for which he served as the model. Mrs. Dennis *(left)* compares the likeness. *Courtesy National Historical Wax Museum*

CENTER, LEFT: Museum visitors and *(from left)* a beefeater at Louis Tussaud's English Wax Museum (Atlantic City), and a bearded sea captain at the Pioneer Square Wax Museum. (Seattle). RIGHT: Here, the author poses at Louis Tussaud's English Wax Museum (Atlantic City) with a likeness of actor Carroll O'Connor, the Archie Bunker of the popular TV series "All in the Family."

LEFT: The attractions at the Movieland Wax Museum begin in the street outside the museum where a wax monster sits in a vintage Rolls-Royce.

BELOW: Representations of five famous men can be seen in the lobby of the Royal London Wax Museum in Phoenix. They are *(from left)* physicist Albert Einstein, inventor Thomas Edison, automaker Henry Ford (in one of his Model T's), humorist Will Rogers, and writer Mark Twain.

TOP TO BOTTOM: The presidents onstage at Walt Disney World's "Hall of Presidents." *Courtesy Walt Disney Productions* President Abraham Lincoln. *Courtesy Walt Disney Productions* Lincoln risen and actually speaking. *Courtesy Walt Disney Productions*

"Audio-Animatronics" in Disneyland and Walt Disney World

Walt Disney was one of those who believed that Americans should understand and appreciate their heritage. He envisioned a special kind of show that would dramatize "in a different and exciting way" the importance of the American heritage to every citizen—in its relationship to the growth and prosperity of the country and in its lasting effect in each personal life.

In 1955, shortly after the opening of Disneyland, plans for an entire area, a whole new "land" were initiated by Disney and his creative staff. A central part of this new land was to be a dramatic presentation of the country's history embodied in the figures of all the past presidents of the United States.

But the figures, once completed, were not successful. Immobile, stiff, they did not reflect the vital energy of the men whose courage shaped America. The only solution was to devise a revolutionary method of three-dimensional animation. Finally, after a number of years of experimentation and trial, there was success with a highly sophisticated new electronics system called "Audio-Animatronics."

Now Disney could proceed. The "land" would be called Liberty Square and the attraction "The Hall of Presidents."

Literally hundreds of Disney artisans, designers, craftsmen, and technicians collaborated on the "The Hall of Presidents." A new five-screen, 70mm cinematic process was created which places the audience in the hypnotic center of the action in a sort of trance, sweeping them into the historic arena where the ethical, idealistic, and Constitutional conflicts of the nation were raised and resolved. The cinematic sequence of the show then deals with the role of justice and science pointing the way to future prosperity and enlightenment.

On this note of optimism, the screen disappears and attention is focused on a curtained stage at the front of the theatre. Slowly, the curtain rises to reveal the shadowed presence of thirty-six lifelike and life-size "audio-animatronics" figures of the United States presidents past. As roll call begins, a spotlight catches the nod of each president. The illusion of reality is again hypnotic on the audience. At the end of the roll call, President Lincoln rises and addresses his colleagues and the audience with his timeless words of wisdom.

Walt Disney's "Audio-Animatronics" system is a front-runner in the modernization of the Tussaud wax technique. Some of the other museums are developing similar automatic techniques. In 1975, the National Historical Wax Museum in Washington, D.C., created an automatic Ben Franklin who speaks to the audience as a master of ceremonies in its Hall of Presidents. Earl Dorfman's Wax Museum Enterprises commercialized this automated process, which includes automated figures in several other wax museums.

2 AMERICAN HISTORY IN WAX

With the exception of those wax museums that specialize in particular areas of interest, such as sports or the movies, American wax museums devote generous exhibit space to historical events and the men and women who participated in them. However, the choice of subjects varies from museum to museum, as does the manner in which events and personages are depicted.

What follows is a selection of exhibits that demonstrates both the extent to which the important events and personages of American history are covered in wax museums and the interesting ways in which American history has been recreated for the museum visitor.

EXPLORERS AND COLONISTS

RIGHT: A tableau set at the Convent of La Rabida shows a figure representing Christopher Columbus *(seated at right)* talking with the Franciscan friars who helped him raise money for his historic voyage to America. A figure of Diego, the eleven-year-old son of Columbus, stands at his right. *Courtesy Miami Wax Museum*

BELOW: The National Historical Wax Museum begins its presentation of historical figures with an effigy of Leif Ericson, the Viking explorer and adventurer who many believe to be the first European to reach North America. It is held that in the year 1000 Ericson landed in the present Nova Scotia, or farther south in North America, after being blown off course on a voyage from Norway to Greenland.

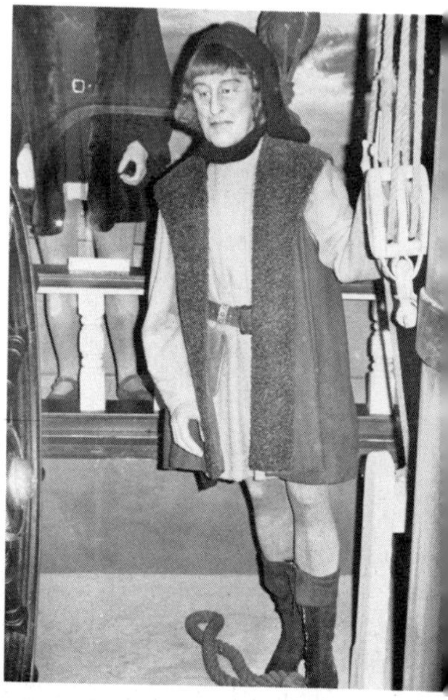

TOP, LEFT: Spanish Queen Isabella, who financed Columbus's voyages of discovery. Louis Tussaud's English Wax Museum (Atlantic City). CENTER: This tableau at the Denver Wax Museum shows Columbus coming ashore at San Salvador. RIGHT: After a grueling fifty-two-day voyage John Cabot reached Cape Breton Island in Nova Scotia in 1497 to lay the foundation for England's claim to North America. He is displayed in a setting that suggests a sailing ship. Royal London Wax Museum (Victoria).

CENTER, LEFT: A tableau re-creates the discovery of Florida by Juan Ponce de León *(center)*. Ponce de León traveled to Florida from Puerto Rico where he had been the Spanish governor. *Courtesy Miami Wax Museum* RIGHT: A legend from Florida's past has been re-created in a tableau that shows the daughter of an Indian chief *(center)* pleading for the life of a young Spaniard named Juan Ortez (with arms tied to tree). Her intervention resulted in Ortez's release. The rescue is reported to have taken place in 1528. *Courtesy Miami Wax Museum*

BOTTOM RIGHT: A tableau re-creates an encounter in 1540 between a band of Spanish explorers led by Hernando DeSoto and a group of Cherokee Indians. It was the Cherokees' first recorded contact with white men. Wax museum of Cherokee History.

TOP, LEFT: The 1579 landing near San Francisco of Sir Francis Drake (with sword). The small inlet where he landed is now called Drake's Bay in honor of the English admiral and buccaneer. *Courtesy Wax Museum at Fisherman's Wharf* RIGHT: In this tableau, Queen Elizabeth I *(left)* is handing Sir Walter Raleigh a charter "to discover barbarous countries." The queen was to receive one-fifth of all precious metals that Raleigh and his associates found in the New World. Williamsburg National Wax Museum.

CENTER, LEFT: Queen Elizabeth I. Royal London Wax Museum (Niagara Falls). CENTER: Sir Walter Raleigh *(kneeling at right)* has brought Queen Elizabeth tobacco and potatoes from America. Louis Tussaud's English Wax Museum (Atlantic City). RIGHT: This rough colonial cabin scene depicts the 1587 christening of Virginia Dare in Sir Walter Raleigh's colony on Roanoke Island in Virginia. Virginia Dare was the first English child born in America. Williamsburg National Wax Museum.

BOTTOM: The first days of the English colony at Jamestown, Virginia, are portrayed in a tableau at the Williamsburg National Wax Museum. One hundred and twenty settlers arrived at Jamestown in May, 1607.

TOP, LEFT: A re-creation of the marriage of Pocahontas *(center)* to John Rolfe, one of the Jamestown colonists *(far left)*. The ceremony took place in April, 1614. American Historical Wax Museum. RIGHT: Pocahontas *(center)* is portrayed as she may have appeared during a visit to the court of King James I in 1616 or 1617. Williamsburg National Wax Museum.

CENTER, LEFT: Jamestown's first House of Representatives met in 1619 in the colony's church. The Williamsburg National Wax Museum has re-created the historic event. RIGHT: This tableau is based on the arrival at Jamestown of the first blacks in 1619. Williamsburg National Wax Museum.

BOTTOM, LEFT: In 1620 the proprietors of Jamestown sent one hundred women to the colony to provide wives for the settlers. Their eagerly awaited landing at Jamestown is the subject of the Williamsburg National Wax Museum tableau seen here. To obtain a wife, a settler had to pay 120 pounds of tobacco. RIGHT: This exhibit illustrates how tobacco was packed in casks for shipment from Jamestown to England. John Rolfe, the husband of Pocahontas, was instrumental in establishing Jamestown's prosperous tobacco trade. Williamsburg National Wax Museum.

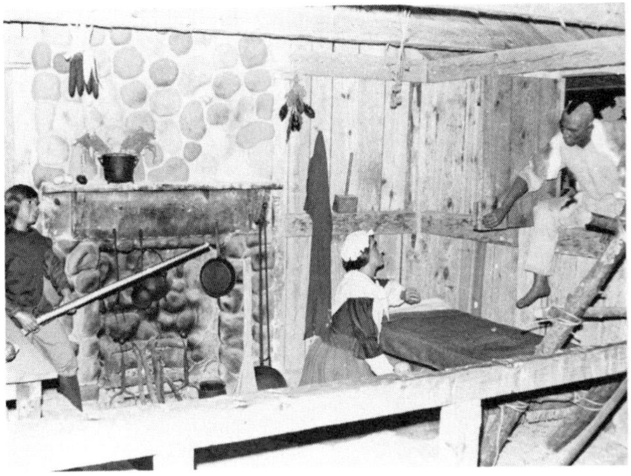

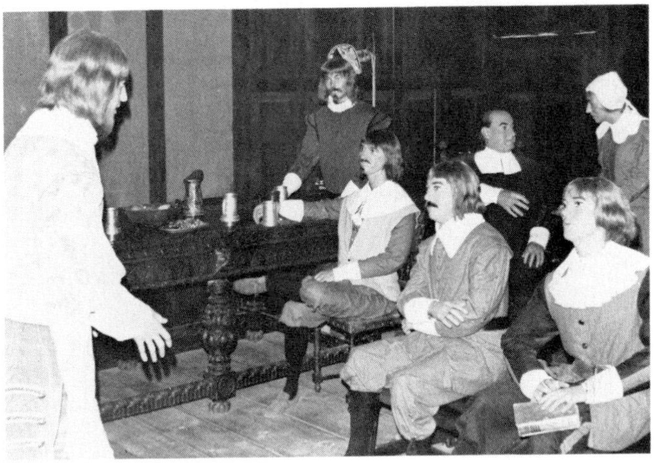

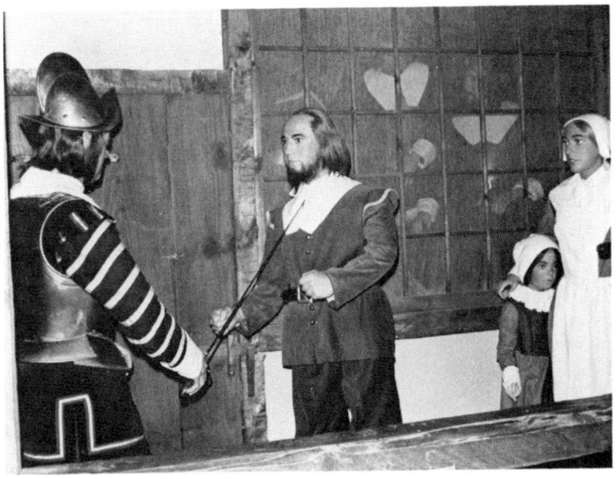

TOP AND CENTER LEFT: In 1622 over 350 colonists in the Jamestown area lost their lives in a surprise Indian attack. These three re-creations of the attack are on display at the Williamsburg National Wax Museum.

CENTER RIGHT: The Plymouth National Wax Museum's portrayal of the coming of the Pilgrims to Plymouth, Massachusetts, begins with a scene set in Scrooby, England, where a group of religious dissenters called Puritans is holding a meeting in a tavern.

BOTTOM, LEFT: In this scene Puritan leader William Brewster *(center)* is being arrested for his religious activities. Plymouth National Wax Museum. RIGHT: Visitors to the Plymouth National Wax Museum next see William Brewster *(left)* in jail. With him are two other Puritan leaders, the Reverend Clyfton *(center)* and John Robinson.

TOP, LEFT: Because of persecution at home, the Scrooby Puritans moved to Holland in 1608. The Plymouth National Wax Museum has re-created their departure from England. RIGHT: This tableau is based on a painting that hangs in the U.S. Capitol. It depicts the Puritans (now called Pilgrims) kneeling in prayer as they begin their journey to America in 1620. Plymouth National Wax Museum.

CENTER, LEFT: Here, a group of Pilgrims is going ashore from the *Mayflower,* anchored in the harbor at Provincetown. The re-creation of the landing is at the Plymouth National Wax Museum. RIGHT: A washday tableau showing Pilgrim women washing clothes after more than two months at sea. Plymouth National Wax Museum.

RIGHT: The Pilgrims' first terrible winter at Plymouth, when disease and hardship wiped out fifty of the one hundred and two *Mayflower* passengers, provides the theme for these dioramas. *Top:* Sick colonists. *Bottom:* A secret nighttime burial to keep the Indians from learning of the colonists' plight. Plymouth National Wax Museum.

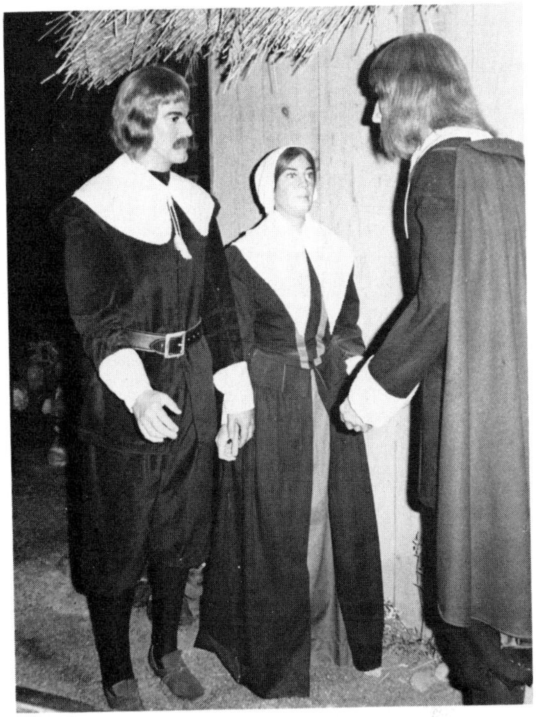

TOP, LEFT: Here, Squanto *(right),* a friendly Indian who spoke English, is showing the Plymouth settlers how to plant corn. The figures are at the Plymouth National Wax Museum. RIGHT: Pilgrim leaders draw up a peace treaty with Massasoit, chief of the Wampanoag Indians. Plymouth National Wax Museum.

SECOND ROW, LEFT: A diorama depicts the devout Pilgrims on their way to church. Plymouth National Wax Museum. RIGHT: The Plymouth colony's first marriage, between the widow Susanna Fuller White and Edward Winslow, took place on May 12, 1621. Plymouth National Wax Museum.

THIRD ROW: According to Henry Wadsworth Longfellow's poem "The Courtship of Miles Standish," Pilgrim John Alden was told to speak for himself when he carried Captain Miles Standish's marriage proposal to Priscilla Mullins. Figures representing John and Priscilla can be seen at the Plymouth National Wax Museum. They were married in 1621 or 1623.

BOTTOM: A scene from the May Day celebration.

TOP, LEFT: In 1635 John Jenney, a brewer, arrived at Plymouth and proposed building a gristmill for the colonists. Jenney is on the right in this model of his gristmill. At left is a likeness of Governor William Bradford. Plymouth National Wax Museum. RIGHT: One of the infamous witch trials held in Salem, Massachusetts, in 1691 and 1692. As many as thirty-two persons accused of witchcraft may have been executed at Salem. National Historical Wax Museum.

CENTER, LEFT: A tableau in the lobby of the Annapolis Naval Historical Wax Museum depicts the departure of the sailing ship *Dove* from England in 1633 carrying colonists who became the first white settlers in Maryland. *Courtesy Annapolis Naval Historical Wax Museum* TOP, RIGHT: Lake George, in the foothills of the Adirondacks in eastern New York State, is believed to have been visited in 1642 by a Jesuit missionary named Isaac Jogues. Waxlife USA has a tableau in which the Jesuit *(center)* and his companions view the lake discovered. (BOTTOM): A re-creation of a visit by Nathaniel Bacon *(right)* to Virginia's Governor Berkeley *(left)* to request protection from Indian raids. The governor's refusal to send help led, in 1676, to Bacon's Rebellion during which Jamestown was burned. Williamsburg National Wax Museum.

LEFT: Blackbeard, the pirate who harassed the Virginia and Carolina coasts from 1716 until 1718, shown in a gory scene at the American Historical Wax Museum. Blackbeard, whose name was Edward Teach, was captured and killed in 1718.

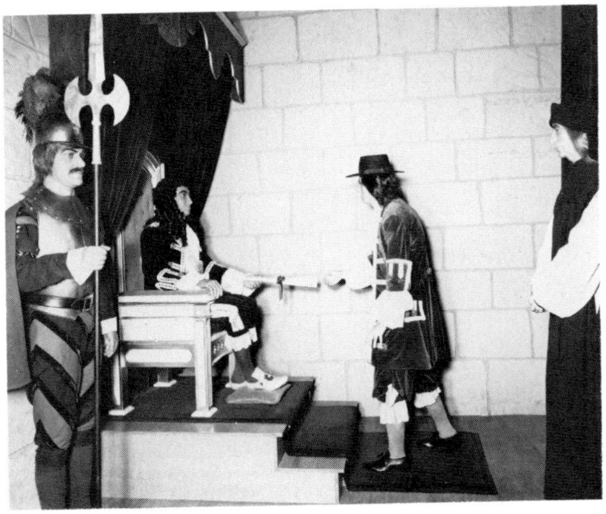

TOP, LEFT: Father Louis Hennepin *(left)* and Robert Cavalier, Sieur de La Salle. In 1675 the two men traveled to Canada on the same ship and Hennepin became La Salle's chaplain. Louis Tussaud's English Wax Museum (Niagara Falls). CENTER: Father Hennepin appears with a group of Indians. The falls of the Niagara River were first described by Hennepin, a Franciscan missionary who saw them in 1678. Burning Springs Wax Museum, Niagara Falls. RIGHT: The Burning Springs Wax Museum's likeness of the explorer La Salle *(right)* is paired with a figure representing Louis de Buade, comte de Palluau et Frontenac, the governor of Canada from 1672 until 1682 and from 1689 to 1698. La Salle claimed Louisiana for King Louis XIV of France.

CENTER, LEFT: Martin Chartier, one of the first white men known to have visited Pennsylvania, trades with Indians for furs. *Courtesy National Wax Museum of Lancaster County Heritage* RIGHT: King Charles II of England formally grants land for a colony to William Penn in this tableau. The land which Penn, a Quaker, acquired in 1681, became Pennsylvania. Penn himself lived there only briefly, from 1682 until 1684 and from 1699 until 1701. *Courtesy National Wax Museum of Lancaster County Heritage*

BOTTOM: Another tableau shows Pennsylvania settlers building a log cabin. *Courtesy National Wax Museum of Lancaster County Heritage*

TOP: The Musée Conti has re-created the meeting in Paris at which plans for the founding of New Orleans were discussed. *Left:* Prince Conti; Minister of Finance John Law; and the Duc d'Orléans, for whom the city was named. CENTER: In 1774 colonial representatives from Pennsylvania, Maryland, and Virginia met with Indian leaders at Lancaster, Pennsylvania, to negotiate a treaty in which the Indians ceded to England their lands north of the Ohio River. *Courtesy National Wax Museum of Lancaster County Heritage* BOTTOM: Benjamin Franklin is purchasing wagons and other supplies for British General Edward Braddock to use in the conflict between Great Britain and France for control of the Ohio River Valley. *Courtesy National Wax Museum of Lancaster County Heritage* RIGHT: General Braddock has been mortally wounded in a battle on July 9, 1775, between the British and a force of French and Indians. Williamsburg National Wax Museum.

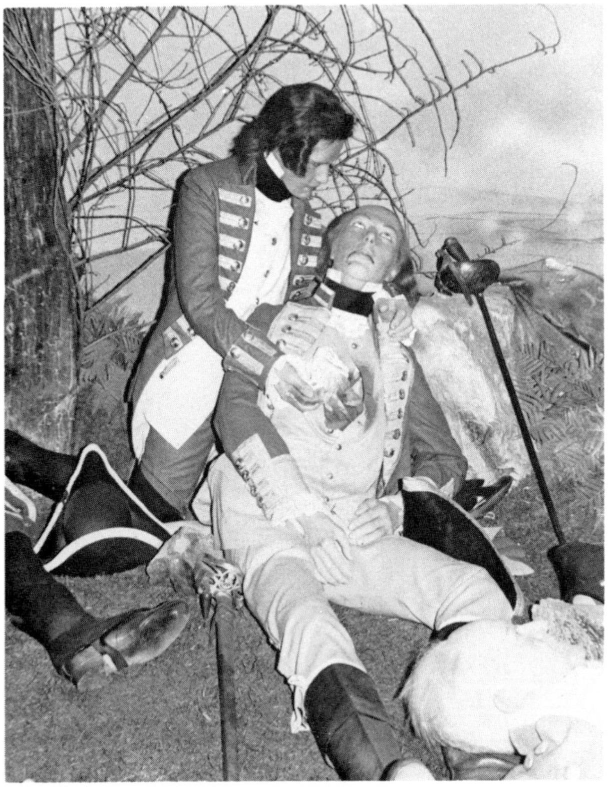

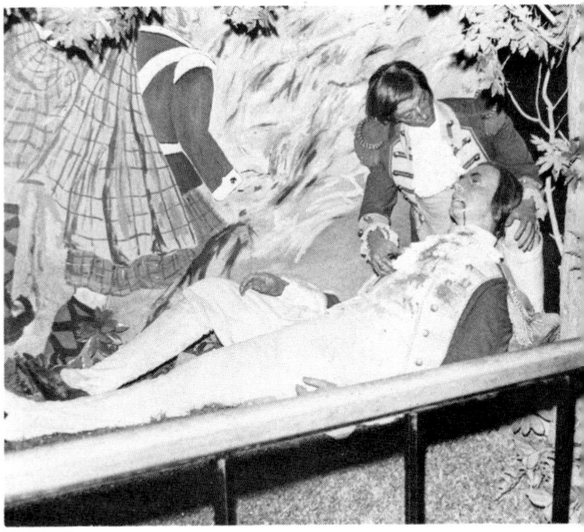

LEFT, TOP: English forces are depicted mounting an attack against the French in the Battle of Lake George in September, 1755. The French suffered a defeat at Lake George. Waxlife USA. CENTER: In this battle scene the English garrison at Fort William Henry, on the shores of Lake George, is surrendering to French General Louis Montcalm and his Indian allies. The year is 1757. Waxlife USA. BOTTOM: Two members of the Scottish Black Watch regiment that helped defeat the French at Ticonderoga. The Black Watch regiment was so named because of the dark colors of its tartan. Waxlife USA.

TOP RIGHT: The bloody battle on the Plains of Abraham, overlooking Quebec, that cost the lives of the opposing generals is the subject of this tableau at the Royal London Wax Museum (Victoria). A figure representing the dying British General James Wolfe lies at center. French General Montcalm died the day after the battle, which was fought on September 13, 1759, and resulted in the surrender of Quebec to the British.

BOTTOM RIGHT: This version of the death of General Wolfe can be seen at the Burning Springs Wax Museum.

THE AMERICAN REVOLUTION

TOP, LEFT: Defender of colonial rights Patrick Henry addressing the Virginia House of Burgesses. In his famous speech to the burgesses Henry urged resistance to the unpopular Stamp Act and used the much quoted words: "If this be treason, make the most of it." Williamsburg National Wax Museum. CENTER: This version of Patrick Henry addressing the House of Burgesses is on view at the American Historical Wax Museum. RIGHT: Massachusetts political leader Samuel Adams. In Massachusetts Adams led the opposition to British rule. Williamsburg National Wax Museum.

CENTER: A re-creation of the Boston Massacre of March 5, 1770, with British troops firing at a group of Bostonians. Williamsburg National Wax Museum.

BOTTOM, LEFT: In December, 1773, when the British East India Company attempted to deliver tea to Boston where the colonials were protesting a tax on tea, a band of residents dressed as Indians dumped the cargo into the harbor. The Williamsburg National Wax Museum re-creates the Boston Tea Party. RIGHT: Colonial Virginia legislators meeting at the Raleigh Tavern where they proposed the organization of a Continental Congress. Williamsburg National Wax Museum.

TOP, LEFT: This scene based on Paul Revere's ride to warn sleeping citizens that British soldiers were marching toward Concord, Massachusetts, is on display at the Williamsburg National Wax Museum. CENTER: One of the casualties of the Boston Museum's Battle of Bunker Hill re-creation. Between 1,000 and 1,500 British soldiers were killed or wounded at Bunker Hill. Although American casualties totaled only 411, the battle was a tactical victory for the British. London Wax Museum of Boston. RIGHT: Ezek Hopkins *(in doorway)*, the first commander of the Navy authorized by the Continental Congress in November, 1775, being introduced by John Adams to members of the Naval Committee in this scene at the Annapolis Naval Historical Wax Museum.

CENTER, LEFT: With the assistance of John Hancock *(right)*, Lieutenant John Paul Jones hoists the Navy's first flag. Annapolis Naval Historical Wax Museum. RIGHT: Betsy Ross appears to be putting the finishing touches on the first American flag. The thirteen-star, thirteen-stripe banner was officially adopted by Congress on June 14, 1777. *Courtesy Miami Wax Museum*

LEFT: Betsy Ross *(right)* shows the completed flag to George and Martha Washington. *Courtesy Shrine to Democracy Wax Museum*

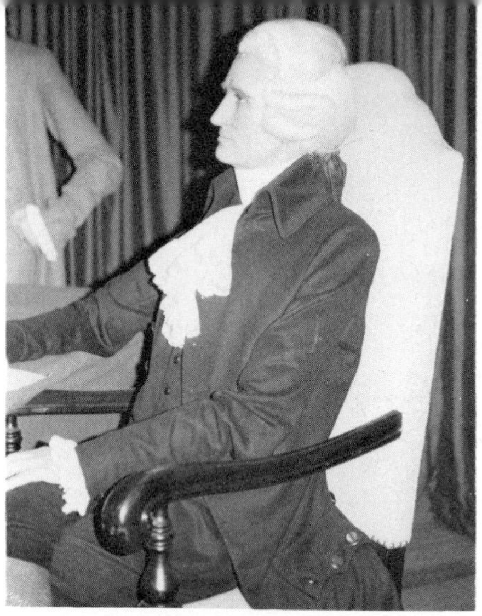

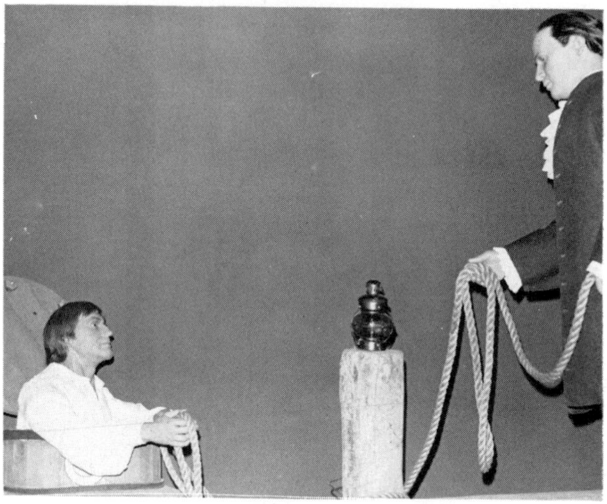

TOP, LEFT: John Hancock *(second from right)* signs the Declaration of Independence while *(left to right)* Benjamin Franklin, Thomas Jefferson, and John Adams look on. National Historical Wax Museum. CENTER: Declaration of Independence signer John Hancock as he appears at Louis Tussaud's English Wax Museum in Atlantic City. RIGHT: The execution of Nathan Hale, the American spy captured by the British in 1776. It was Hale who said: "I only regret that I have but one life to lose for my country." American Historical Wax Museum.

CENTER, LEFT: Benedict Arnold *(right)*, who later turned traitor, was still loyal to the American cause in this scene. The tableau is based on Arnold's attempt to stop a fleet of British warships from advancing southward on Lake Champlain in the fall of 1776. Although Arnold lost the Battle of Valcour Bay, he delayed British invasion plans for a year. *Courtesy Annapolis Naval Historical Wax Museum* RIGHT: One of maritime history's important firsts, the operational submarine, is the subject of this scene at the Annapolis Naval Historical Wax Museum. Developed by David and Ezra Bushnell, the submarine made several unsuccessful attacks on British ships in New York Harbor during the fall of 1776. The British called the sub a "devilish product of Yankee engineering."

BOTTOM, LEFT: The Hall of American Presidents Wax Museum presents General George Washington's famous crossing of the Delaware River on December 25, 1776, to lead a successful attack on the Hessians at Trenton, New Jersey. RIGHT: In this scene church members, who have been informed that the British are about to invade Pennsylvania, meet with their pastor in the churchyard. *Courtesy National Wax Museum of Lancaster Country Heritage*

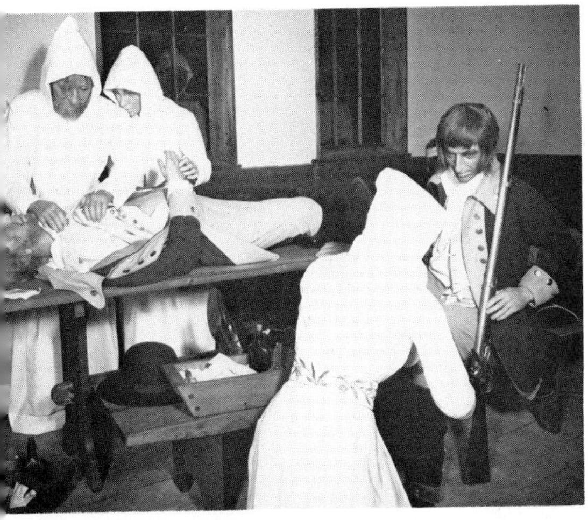

TOP, LEFT: This unusual tableau based on local history shows members of a cloistered Seventh-Day Baptist sect caring for wounded soldiers from the Battle of Brandywine. *Courtesy National Wax Museum of Lancaster County Heritage* RIGHT: On September 27, 1777, the Continental Congress, forced to flee from British-occupied Philadelphia, met for one day at Lancaster, Pennsylvania, as seen here. *Courtesy National Wax Museum of Lancaster County Heritage*

CENTER, LEFT: In a snow-filled scene at the American Army's encampment at Valley Forge during the winter of 1777-78, General George Washington kneels in prayer. The Valley Forge re-creation is at Seattle's Pioneer Square Wax Museum. CENTER: Molly Pitcher, the heroine of the Battle of Monmouth, is honored with this tableau. Molly, whose real name was Mary Hays, replaced her gunner husband in a major battle that ended in a British withdrawal to New York City. Williamsburg National Wax Museum. RIGHT: John Paul Jones, American naval hero of the Revolutionary War, appears on the deck of his flagship, the *Bonhomme Richard,* in a spectacular sound and light tableau at the Annapolis Naval Historical Wax Museum. Jones uttered the famous words: "I have not yet begun to fight" in September, 1779, when he was asked to surrender the *Bonhomme Richard* to the stronger British warship *Serapis.* After a bitter three-and-one-half-hour struggle Jones forced the *Serapis* to surrender.

BOTTOM, LEFT: The meeting on the night of September 21, 1780, between traitor Benedict Arnold *(left)* and British Major John André. After the meeting, André was captured and hanged as a spy. Arnold, who had agreed to surrender the American fort at West Point, New York, to the British, escaped. He died in England in 1801. Seattle's Pioneer Square Wax Museum. RIGHT: Major André when he was an interned prisoner living in a Lancaster County home during the first year of the War for Independence. He was released in a prisoner exchange at the end of 1776. *Courtesy National Wax Museum of Lancaster County Heritage*

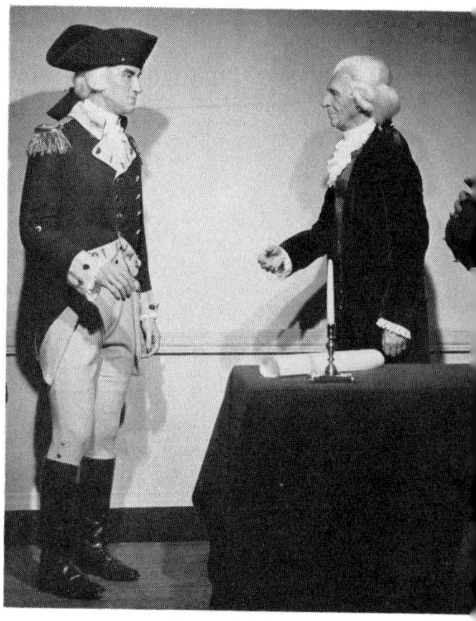

TOP, LEFT: The visit of American envoy Benjamin Franklin *(seated)* to the Trianon Palace at Versailles. He is with the Marquis de Lafayette. Musée Historique, Quebec. RIGHT: Trianon Palace tableau showing Queen Marie Antoinette and King Louis XVI in the Musee Historique.

CENTER PAGE: The Marquis de Lafayette wears a uniform similar to the one he wore while fighting for the American cause during the Revolution. Lafayette, who was nineteen when he arrived in America, became a lifelong friend of George Washington. Musée Conti.

LEFT, TOP: A dramatic scene from the Battle of Yorktown. In October, 1781, at Yorktown in southeastern Virginia, American troops with the help of their French allies decisively defeated the British and ended the Revolutionary War. Williamsburg National Wax Museum. BOTTOM: Another portion of the Williamsburg tableau.

ABOVE, RIGHT: George Washington *(left)* tenders his resignation as commander in chief of the Continental Army to the Continental Congress, then meeting at Annapolis, Maryland. The resignation ceremony, a tearful one, took place on December 23, 1783. *Courtesy Annapolis Naval Historical Wax Museum*

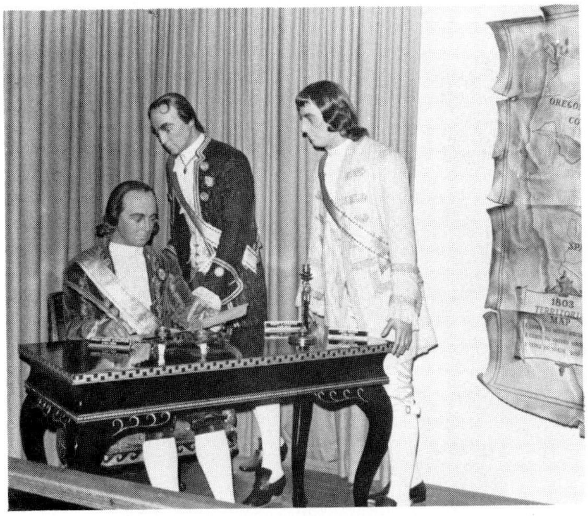

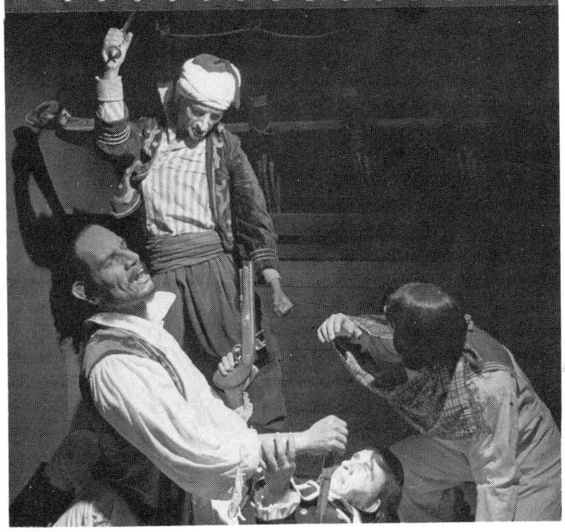

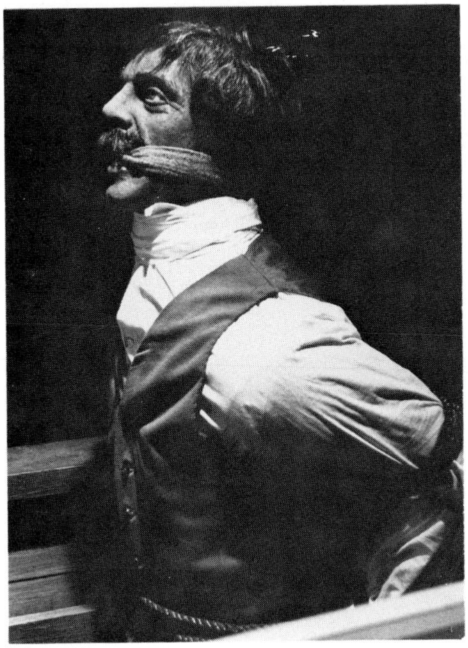

A NEW NATION

TOP, LEFT: Frontiersman and hunter Daniel Boone, who began his exploration of what is now Kentucky in 1767, is posed at the American Historical Wax Museum with a newly killed bear. RIGHT: Spanish soldiers confront two Americans *(left)* attempting to unload cargo at New Orleans in this scene at the Musée Conti. The Spanish ceded Louisiana to France in 1800.

CENTER, LEFT: The Denver Wax Museum's Louisiana Purchase tableau includes figures of *(from left)* Robert R. Livingston, the American minister to France; James Monroe, minister extraordinary who served with Livingston; and French statesman and diplomat Talleyrand. CENTER: In May, 1804, Meriwether Lewis and William Clark started up the Missouri River to begin their two-year exploration of the West. The National Historical Wax Museum includes Sacajawea *(center),* the Indian girl who helped guide the explorers, in its Lewis and Clark exhibit. RIGHT: U.S. Army officer Zebulon Pike in full uniform. He discovered the Rocky Mountains peak that bears his name in 1806. Denver's Wax Museum.

BOTTOM, LEFT: The bound and gagged figure represents an American seaman who has been forcibly removed from his ship for service with the British navy. The unlawful seizure of American seamen by the British was one of the reasons that the United States declared war on Great Britain in 1812. The scene is at the Annapolis Naval Historical Wax Museum. ABOVE: American seamen also encountered trouble in the Mediterranean Sea where the Barbary pirates attacked U.S. shipping. In this pirate attack in 1804 Seaman Daniel Frazier *(right)* saved the life of Lieutenant Stephen Decatur. *Courtesy Annapolis Naval Historical Wax Museum*

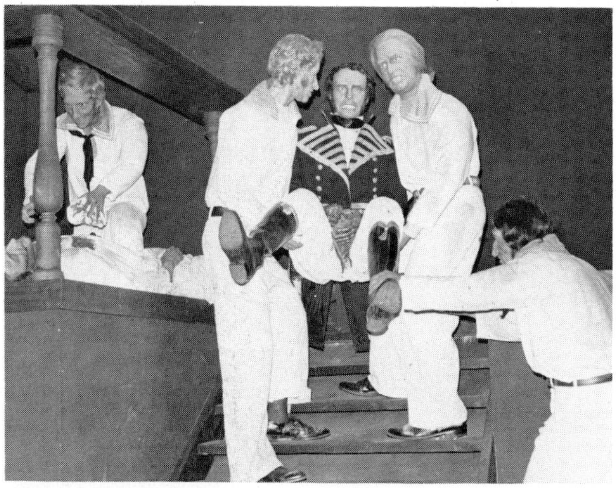

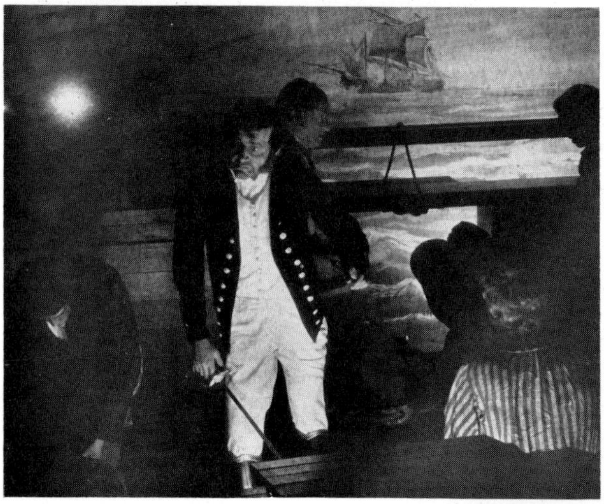

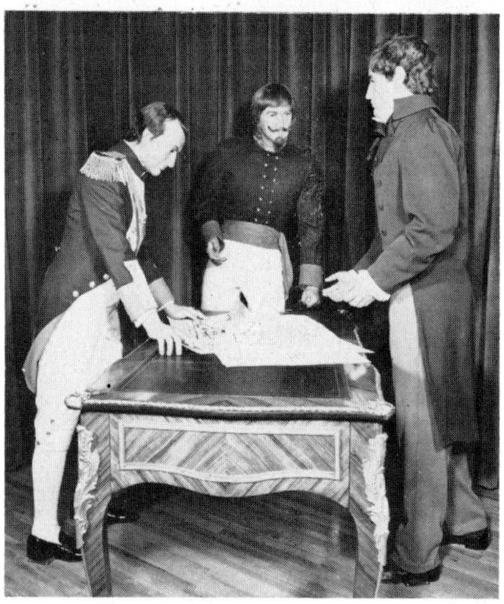

TOP, LEFT: The death of British General Sir Isaac Brock during an American attack on Queenston in southern Canada in October, 1812, is re-created here. In spite of Brock's death, the American forces were able to hold Queenston for only a few hours. Louis Tussaud's English Wax Museum (Niagara Falls).

CENTER, TOP: Mortally wounded, Capt. James Lawrence is helped from the deck of the American ship *Chesapeake* after an encounter in 1813 with the British ship *Shannon*. Before he died, Lawrence told his men: "Don't give up the ship!" Annapolis Naval Historical Wax Museum. BOTTOM: Special sound and light effects add a realistic touch to a re-creation of the Battle of Lake Erie in which defiant Captain Oliver Hazard Perry stands on the deck of his ship during the Battle of Lake Erie. After Perry's hard-fought victory over the British Lake Erie fleet, he reported to his superior: "We have met the enemy and they are ours." *Courtesy Annapolis Naval Historical Wax Museum*

RIGHT, TOP: Francis Scott Key composes the words of "The Star Spangled Banner." Key, a Lawyer, wrote the famous lyrics in 1814 while being held aboard a British ship during the bombardment of Fort McHenry in Baltimore harbor. Miami Wax Museum. CENTER: Robert Fulton *(right)*, a native of Lancaster County, Pennsylvania, showing a drawing of his submarine to Napoleon Bonaparte. During the War of 1812 Fulton constructed a floating fort for the defense of New York harbor. *Courtesy National Wax Museum of Lancaster County Heritage* BOTTOM: British plans for the capture of New Orleans could be the subject under discussion in this tableau representing General Andrew Jackson *(left)* and pirate leader Jean Lafitte. Lafitte, who had been offered a large sum of money by the British for his help, aided the Americans in return for a pardon for himself and his men. National Historical Wax Museum.

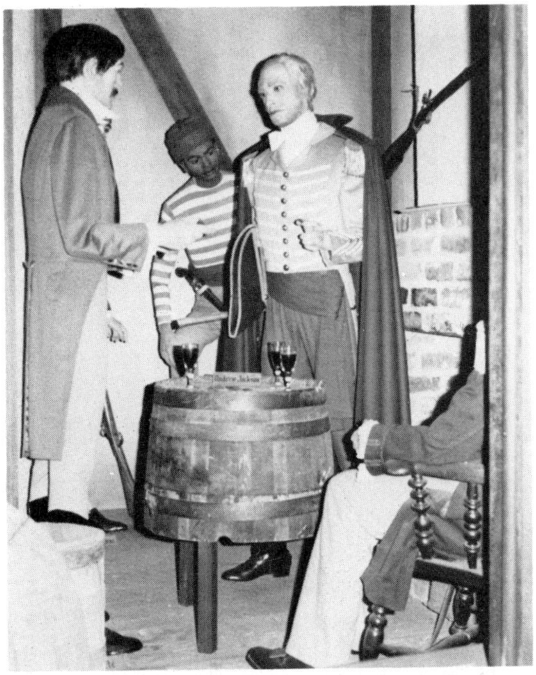

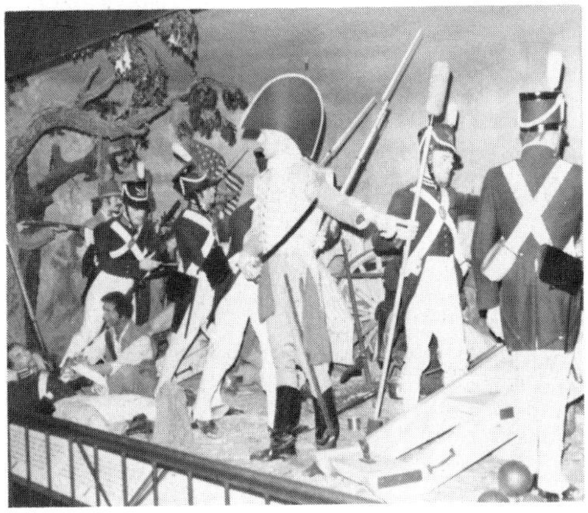

TOP, LEFT: At the Musée Conti General Jackson *(seated)* and Jean Lafitte *(center)* in Lafitte's blacksmith shop, supposed to have been located on New Orlean's Bourbon Street. The figure on the left represents Louisiana Governor William Claiborne. RIGHT: Pirate Jean Lafitte *(right)* and General Andrew Jackson appear to be discussing tactics in a tableau based on the Battle of New Orleans. With the help of Lafitte and his men, Jackson defeated the British on January 8, 1815, in the last major engagement of the War of 1812. American Historical Wax Museum.

CENTER, ABOVE: The Musée Conti's largest tableau recreates the Battle of New Orleans, which was fought fifteen days after the signing of the Treaty of Ghent that ended the War of 1812. *Left:* General Jackson directs his men. *Right:* Two of Jackson's soldiers.

CENTER, LEFT: Battle of New Orleans hero Jean Lafitte *(right)* in a setting that suggests Lafitte's pirate headquarters. *Courtesy Southwestern Historical Wax Museum*

BOTTOM: Jean Lafitte in a swashbuckling pose. After the Battle of New Orleans he resumed privateering against the Spanish. *Courtesy Shrine to Democracy Wax Museum*

TOP, LEFT: Texas hero Jim Bowie *(right)* in a replica of the legendary lost San Saba silver mine. At left is a figure representing Indian Chief Xolic who is supposed to have taken Bowie to the mine. Hall of Texas History Wax Museum. TOP, RIGHT: The Battle of the Alamo. *Courtesy Miami Wax Museum* CENTER: In this Battle of the Alamo tableau are *(from left)* Jim Bowie (ill and in bed), James Bonham, William Travis, and Davy Crockett. They and the rest of the outnumbered Alamo garrison perished when the Mexicans breached the fort's walls on March 6, 1836. *Courtesy Southwestern Historical Wax Museum*

ABOVE, LEFT: A close-up of Sam Houston in the Hall of Texas History. In 1836 Houston became the first president of the Republic of Texas. Out of favor during the Civil War because of his anti-Confederacy views, Houston has since regained his First Citizen of Texas status. RIGHT: Sam Houston, with Davy Crockett at the Wax Museum of Cherokee History. At one time Houston lived with the Cherokee Indians.

BOTTOM: A Comanche raid on a Texas homestead. Hall of Texas History.

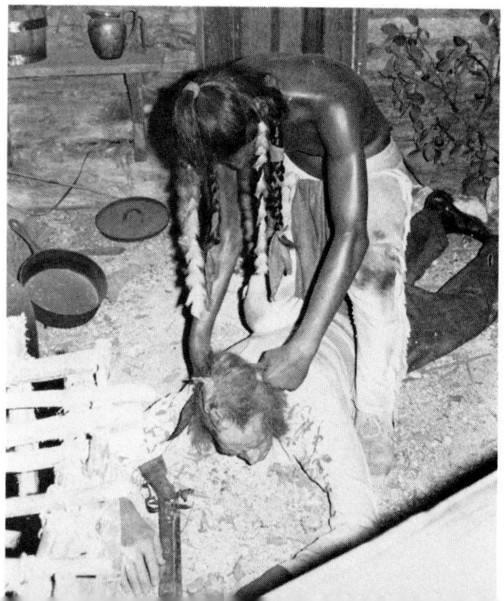

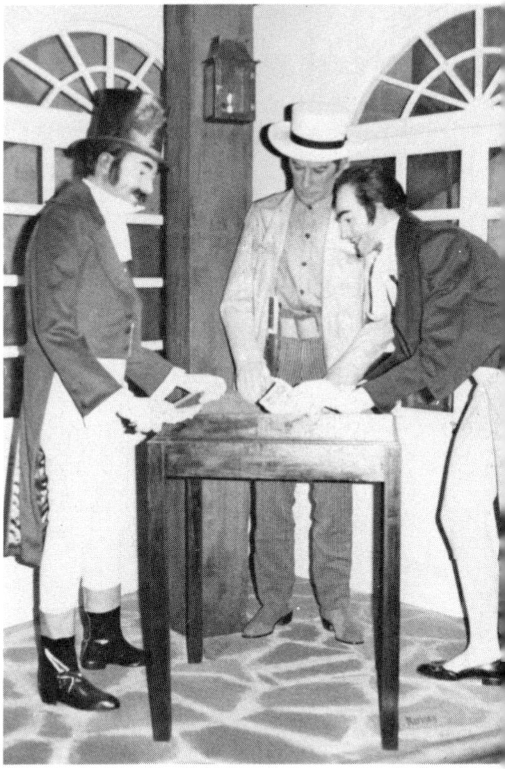

TOP, LEFT: Portrayal of an Indian raid. *Courtesy Tokyo Tower Wax Museum*
RIGHT: Florida's Seminole Indians are remembered with a figure of the young Chief Osceola. The figure has been placed in a replica of the cell at Fort Moultrie in Charleston, South Carolina, where Osceola died in 1838 following his capture during the Second Seminole War. *Courtesy Miami Wax Museum*

CENTER, LEFT: Sequoyah, who is credited with devising the Cherokee alphabet of 56 letters. Wax Museum of Cherokee History. CENTER: A close-up from the Robert E. Lee—Indian village tableau at the Hall of Texas History. Before the Civil War Lee served on the Texas frontier. RIGHT: Craps, a gambling game said to have been introduced to the United States by a citizen of New Orleans, is the subject of this tableau. Musée Conti.

BOTTOM: Voodooism came to New Orleans in the early 1800s by way of the West Indies. These are voodoo dancers at the Musée Conti.

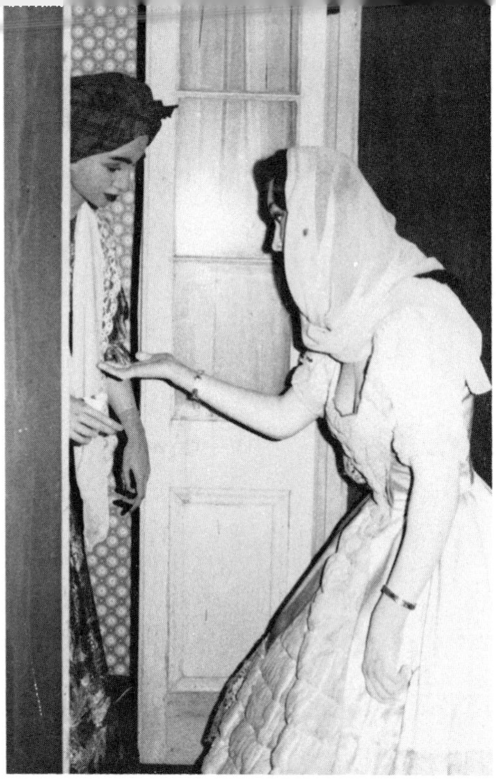

TOP, LEFT: Marie Laveau *(left)* was a famous voodoo queen who practiced her art in New Orleans until her death in 1881. She is shown receiving a client. Musée Conti. RIGHT: New Orleans opened its first theatre in 1792. In this tableau the singer Jenny Lind sits in a box at the left. *Right:* John Wilkes Booth and Sarah Bernhardt. Musée Conti.

CENTER, LEFT: Mormon leader Brigham Young *(right)* and some of his followers reach Great Salt Lake. When the Mormons arrived there in 1847, the area was Mexican territory. Denver Wax Museum. RIGHT: Joshua Abraham Norton, one of California's "Forty-Niners," stayed on in San Francisco to proclaim himself Norton I, Emperor of the United States and Protector of Mexico. Norton I is seen in "royal" garb. *Courtesy Wax Museum at Fisherman's Wharf*

BOTTOM, LEFT: Chief Seattle *(center)*, for whom the City of Seattle was named, appears with Seattle settlers Dr. David Maynard *(left)* and Isaac Stevens, the first Governor of Washington Territory. Pioneer Square Wax Museum. BELOW: *From left:* John Low, D. T. Denny, and Leander Terry, the men who chose the site for Seattle. Pioneer Square Wax Museum.

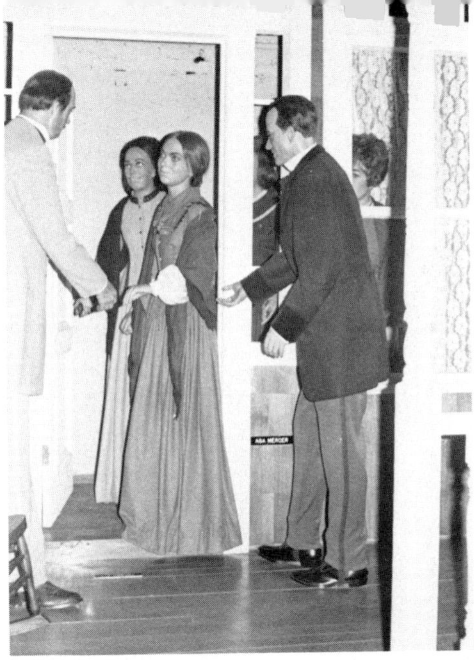

TOP, LEFT: The construction of Seattle's first sawmill, which began operation in 1853. Pioneer Square Wax Museum. RIGHT: Standing in the doorway are two of Seattle's "Mercer Girls," young women brought to Seattle by Asa Mercer in 1864 and 1865 to increase the city's supply of marriageable females. Pioneer Square Wax Museum.

CENTER, LEFT: Ouray *(standing)* was a powerful chief of the Utes whose friendship helped Colorado's settlers. Denver Wax Museum. RIGHT: Other Coloradians honored at Denver Wax Museum include *(from left)* Baby Doe Tabor, a Colorado legend who once enjoyed immense wealth from silver mines, but died penniless; and Margaret Brown, who struck it rich with a silver mine and whose life provided the story line for the musical comedy *The Unsinkable Molly Brown.*

LEFT, TOP: American ships can be seen in the background of this tableau recreating Commodore Matthew Perry's landing in Japan to negotiate a treaty between that country and the United States. *Courtesy Tokyo Tower Wax Museum* BOTTOM: Commodore Perry presents a letter from President Millard Fillmore to Prince Idzu, the Japanese emperor's representative. In 1854 Perry's diplomatic efforts were rewarded with a treaty that opened two Japanese ports to the United States. Annapolis Naval Historical Wax Museum.

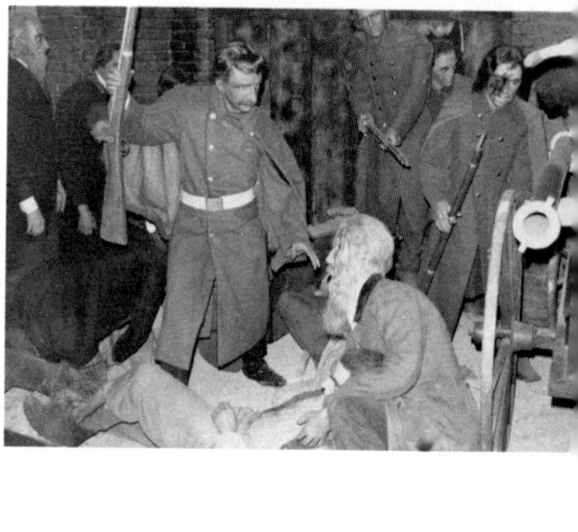

A DIVIDED NATION

TOP: Union and Confederate flags decorate the façade of the National Civil War Wax Museum in Gettysburg, Pennsylvania. The exhibits here have been designed to acquaint visitors with the causes of the Civil War and the men and women who were involved in that conflict.

SECOND ROW: The National Civil War Wax Museum symbolizes the life-styles of the North and the South that led to the outbreak of the Civil War. *Left:* A garment factory in the industrialized North. *Right:* A pastoral scene typical of the antebellum South.

THIRD ROW, LEFT: Eli Whitney operates a model of the cotton gin that he patented in 1794. The gin (short for engine) made cotton production with slave labor more profitable. National Civil War Wax Museum. CENTER: A slave auction in New Orleans during the 1840s when the city's St. Louis Exchange Hotel was the site of daily sales. Musée Conti. RIGHT: Harriet Beecher Stowe, foe of slavery. Mrs. Stowe's *Uncle Tom's Cabin,* published in 1852, helped to arouse antislavery feeling in the North. National Civil War Wax Museum.

BOTTOM: U.S. troops, commanded by Colonel Robert E. Lee, force John Brown and his men to surrender. At center Brown kneels over his dying son Oliver. John Brown Wax Museum.

TOP, LEFT: John Brown's execution at Burning Springs Wax Museum.
CENTER: Southern leader Robert B. Rhett, who advocated secession of the Southern states from the Union. National Civil War Wax Museum.
RIGHT: As a representative and senator from Kentucky during the decades before the Civil War, Henry Clay worked to save the Union. His wax likeness can be seen at the National Civil War Wax Museum.

CENTER, LEFT: Figures representing Confederate General Pierre Beauregard *(right)* and Southern leader Edmund Ruffin appear to be conferring in this scene. Major Robert Anderson can be seen in the light show part of this exhibit (here just starting to appear). On April 14, 1861, Anderson was forced to surrender Fort Sumter at Charleston, South Carolina, to Southern forces. Beauregard ordered the bombardment that led to the surrender of Fort Sumter and Ruffin fired the first shot at the fort from nearby Morris Island. National Civil War Wax Museum. RIGHT: General Beauregard. Musée Conti.

BOTTOM: Shocked by the suffering of wounded Civil War soldiers, Clara Barton received permission to distribute supplies to them and she assisted the wounded in an unofficial capacity for the duration of the war. This portrayal of Clara Barton caring for wounded soldiers can be seen at the American Historical Wax Museum.

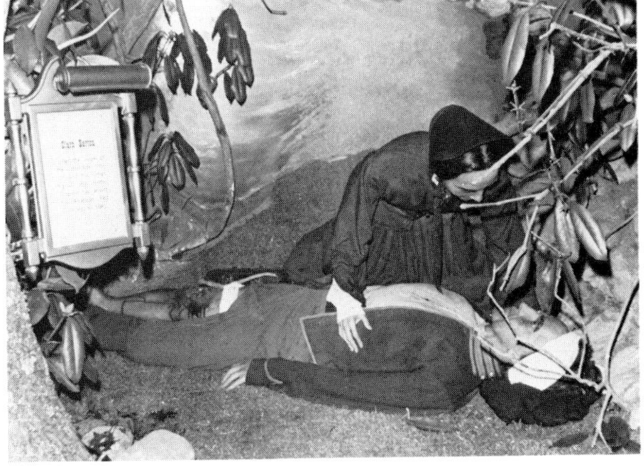

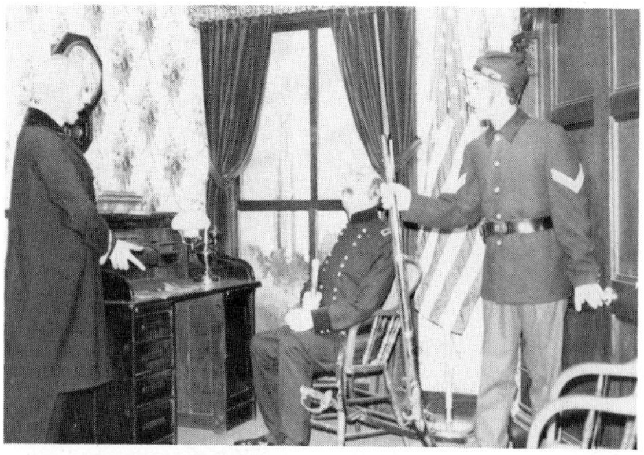

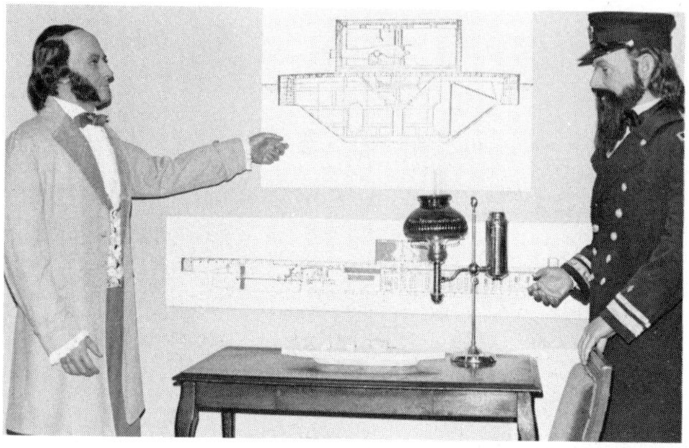

TOP, LEFT: Union General Benjamin Butler *(center)*, administrator of New Orleans after its capture in 1862, shares an office setting with Father James Mullen *(left)*. When asked to bury a dead Union soldier, Father Mullen, a Southern sympathizer, is supposed to have told General Butler that he would gladly bury the whole Union army. Musée Conti. RIGHT: On March 8, 1862, the *Monitor* and the Confederate ironclad *Merrimac* fought the first naval engagement between armored ships. The result was inconclusive. John Erickson *(left)* explains his *Monitor* design to its captain. Annapolis Naval Historical Wax Museum.

CENTER, LEFT: Characters in John Greenleaf Whittier's poem, "Barbara Frietchie." Union sympathizer Barbara Frietchie displays the American flag at a second-story window while *(below)* Confederate General Stonewall Jackson appears to be saying: "Who touches a hair of yon gray head dies like a dog!" American Historical Wax Museum. RIGHT: A Union soldier appears to be explaining Lincoln's Emancipation Proclamation to a black couple. The presidential proclamation freeing the slaves was issued on January 1, 1863. Burning Springs Wax Museum.

BOTTOM, LEFT: Confederate spy Belle Boyd confronts a Union soldier at the National Civil War Wax Museum. Belle Boyd is credited with obtaining much useful information for the South during the early months of the Civil War. She later became a successful actress. CENTER: President Abraham Lincoln with three of his generals at the National Historical Wax Museum. *From left:* William Tecumseh Sherman, George Armstrong Custer, Lincoln, and George B. McClellan. RIGHT: General Ulysses S. Grant, who assumed command of all the Union armies in March, 1864, is posed beside a Civil War cannon at Atlanta's Underground Wax Museum. Grant, a West Point graduate, was forced to resign from the Army in 1854 because of heavy drinking. In 1861 he resumed his military career as the commander of an Illinois volunteer regiment.

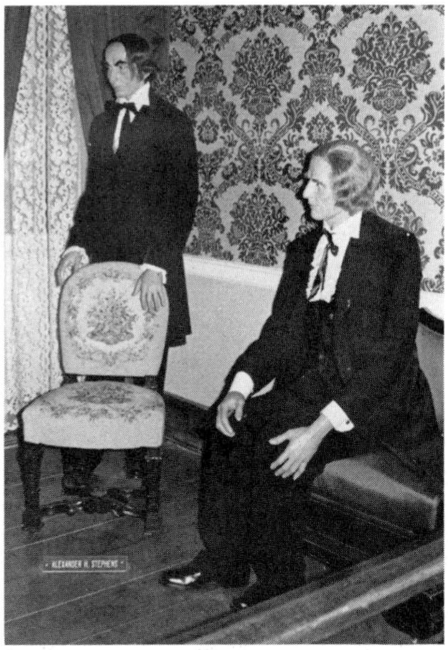

TOP, LEFT: Two of the North's civilian wartime leaders: Secretary of State William Seward *(seated)* and Secretary of War Edwin M. Stanton. National Civil War Wax Museum. CENTER: Jefferson Davis *(seated)* with the vice-president of the Confederacy, Alexander Stephens, at the National Civil War Wax Museum. Following his graduation from West Point, Davis served in the U.S. Army for seven years. Later he represented Mississippi in the House of Representatives and in the Senate and he was President Franklin Pierce's Secretary of War. Davis was imprisoned for two years after the Civil War. Stephens, who weighed only ninety pounds, was nicknamed "Little Allick." RIGHT: Jefferson Davis *(right)* with *(from left)* General Robert E. Lee and General Stonewall Jackson. *Courtesy Miami Wax Museum*

CENTER, LEFT: At the outbreak of the Civil War Confederate General Robert E. Lee was offered the command of Union troops in the field, but he chose to resign his U.S. Army commission to serve the South. Mammoth Cave Wax Museum. RIGHT: A snow-covered command post provides an authentic background for the National Civil War Wax Museum's figures of Civil War generals. *From left:* John Mosby, Jubal Early, Jeb Stuart, and Nathan B. Forrest.

BOTTOM: Summer foliage surrounds a meeting of Southern military leaders. The generals are *(from left)* Nathan B. Forrest, Joseph Johnston, James Longstreet, and Jeb Stuart. American Historical Wax Museum.

TOP, LEFT: Stonewall Jackson lies mortally wounded by fire from his own forces during the Battle of the Wilderness. The death of one of its most brilliant tacticians on May 5, 1863, was a severe blow to the South. National Civil War Wax Museum. CENTER: General George Meade, the commander of the Union forces at the Battle of Gettysburg, posed in a battlefield hut. Meade, who over his own objections assumed command just a week before the battle, managed to defeat the more experienced General Robert E. Lee. National Civil War Wax Museum. RIGHT: Using a quill pen, President Abraham Lincoln appears to be composing a speech at Louis Tussaud's English Wax Museum (Atlantic City). Lincoln's most famous speech, his Gettysburg Address, was delivered on November 19, 1863, at the dedication of the national cemetery on the Gettysburg battlefield.

CENTER, LEFT: George Armstrong Custer as a Civil War cavalry officer. Custer, who was graduated last in the class of 1861 at West Point, was a major general when the Civil War ended. National Civil War Wax Museum. CENTER: Admiral David G. Farragut, responsible for important Union victories at New Orleans and Mobile Bay, on shipboard at the National Civil War Wax Museum. Farragut became a Navy midshipman at the age of nine. RIGHT: Atlanta, an important Confederate supply and communications center, burns in the background at the Underground Wax Museum. Union forces set fire to the central portion of Atlanta on November 12, 1864, after the city's defenders had abandoned it.

BOTTOM: With the acceptance of surrender terms by Confederate General Robert E. Lee at Appomattox Court House on April 9, 1865, the Civil War came to an end. Included in the surrender agreement was the provision that each Confederate soldier "will be allowed to return to his home." Also, if he owned a horse, he could take it home with him. General Lee (in light-colored uniform) is here going over the surrender terms with General Ulysses S. Grant at the National Historical Wax Museum.

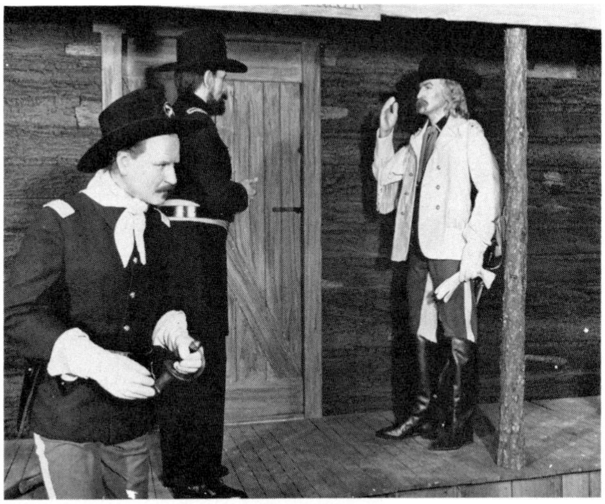

LIFE IN THE OLD WEST

TOP, LEFT: A historic Indian war council features Sioux leaders *(from left)* Gall, Crazy Horse, Rain-in-the-Face, and Sitting Bull, all of whom cooperated in the action that led to the annihilation of U.S. Army forces under General George Armstrong Custer at Little Bighorn in northern Wyoming on June 25, 1876. *Courtesy Shrine to Democracy Wax Museum* RIGHT: Custer *(right)* appears with fellow 7th Cavalry officers *(from left)* Major Marcus Reno and General Alfred H. Terry. *Courtesy Shrine to Democracy Wax Museum*

CENTER, LEFT: General Custer *(center)* lies with the bodies of two of his men in the Denver Wax Museum's "Custer's Last Stand" tableau. Custer's entire command of 655 men was wiped out by the Sioux. RIGHT: Apache Chief Geronimo, who led devastating raids on both sides of the Mexican border, sits in his tent at the Mammoth Cave Wax Museum. Geronimo's reign of terror in the Southwest ended with his capture in 1886 by U.S. Army forces.

BOTTOM, LEFT: Buffalo Bill as the impresario of his "Wild West Show," opened in 1883. Denver Wax Museum. CENTER: Annie Oakley shares the stage with two famous western characters, Calamity Jane *(left)* and Wild Bill Hickok. Potter's Wax Museum. RIGHT: The famous gunfight at the O.K. Corral in Tombstone, Arizona, on October 26, 1881. *From left:* Doc Holliday, Morgan Earp, Virgil Earp, Tombstone jail escapee Frank McLaury, and Wyatt Earp. Stretched out in the foreground is Tom McLaury, another escapee from the Tombstone jail. The showdown at the O.K. Corral resulted in the return of law and order to Tombstone. *Courtesy Southwestern Historical Wax Museum*

TOP, LEFT: The poker game that ended with the shooting of frontier marshal and scout Wild Bill Hickok *(center)*. The game took place in a saloon and gambling hall at Deadwood, Dakota Territory, in 1876. *Courtesy Southwestern Historical Wax Museum* RIGHT: Notorious western outlaws *(from left)* Frank James, William Clarke Quantrill, Jesse James, and Cole Younger are posed outside a bank at the Southwestern Historical Wax Museum.

CENTER, LEFT: A western courtroom of the 1800s is background for Judge Isaac Parker, "The Hanging Judge," and Belle Starr, "Queen of the Bandits." Belle was sentenced to a year in prison by Judge Parker. *Courtesy Southwestern Historical Wax Museum* CENTER: Belle Starr at the Mammoth Cave Wax Museum. The Queen of the Bandits was killed by an unknown assailant in 1889. RIGHT: Calamity Jane (Martha Jane Burke) at the Royal London Wax Museum in Phoenix. The famous frontierswoman, who often dressed as a man, was an excellent sharpshooter. At various times she worked as an Indian fighter and as an army scout.

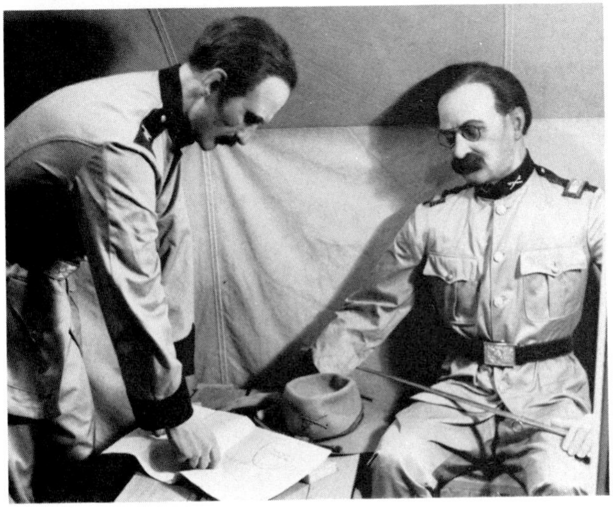

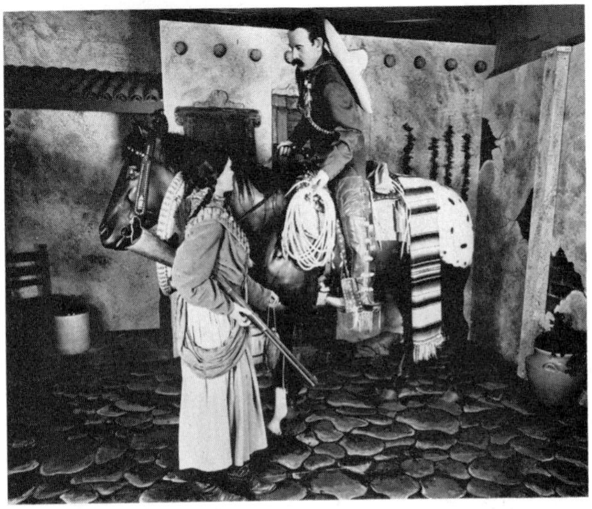

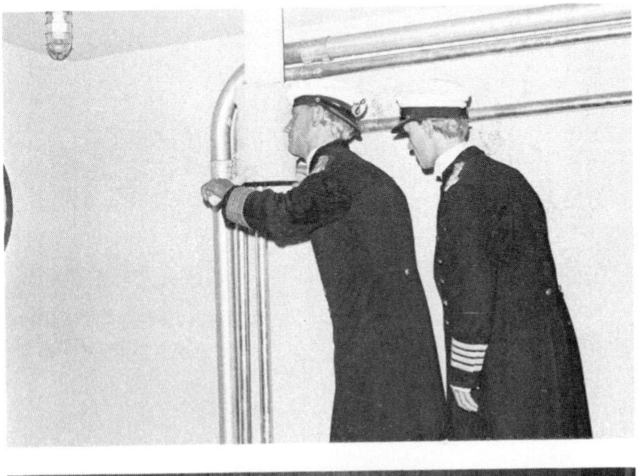

THE UNITED STATES AT WAR

TOP, LEFT: Two figures representing American sailors appear to fly through the bulkhead of the exploding battleship *Maine.* The destruction of the *Maine* in the harbor at Havana, Cuba, on February 15, 1898, led to the Spanish-American War. *Courtesy Annapolis Naval Historical Wax Museum* RIGHT: Theodore Roosevelt *(left)* interviews two prospective members of the First Regiment of U.S. Volunteer Cavalry, an organization that trained in Texas in May, 1898, and later won fame in Cuba as the Rough Riders. Roosevelt, a future president of the United States, was second in command of the Rough Riders. Hall of Texas History Wax Museum.

CENTER, LEFT: Lieutenant Colonel Roosevelt *(right)* appears with the commander of the Rough Riders, Colonel Leonard Wood, in a setting that represents a headquarters tent in Cuba. Forced to leave their horses behind when they embarked for Cuba, the Rough Riders made their celebrated attack on San Juan Hill as foot soldiers. *Courtesy Miami Wax Museum* RIGHT: When Mexican revolutionary leader Francisco "Pancho" Villa invaded New Mexico in 1916, he was driven back by an American expeditionary force. *Courtesy Southwestern Historical Wax Museum*

THIRD ROW: A German submarine officer uses a periscope while a fellow officer looks on in a tableau based on the sinking of the *Lusitania* during World War I. The *Lusitania* carried 1,198 passengers, 124 of them Americans, when she was torpedoed and sunk off the Irish coast in May, 1915. Annapolis Naval Historical Wax Museum.

BOTTOM: World War I hero Sergeant Alvin C. York appears in action at the American Historical Wax Museum. York, a sharpshooter from Tennessee, won the Medal of Honor for his capture of 132 German prisoners.

TOP, LEFT: World War I leaders *(from left)* Georges Clemenceau, Premier of France; Marshal Ferdinand Foch, Commander-in-Chief of Allied Forces; and American General John J. Pershing. Miami Wax Museum. RIGHT: In this World War II tableau a family gathers around a radio to hear news of the Japanese attack on Pearl Harbor on December 7, 1941. *Courtesy Annapolis Naval Historical Wax Museum*

CENTER, LEFT: President Franklin D. Roosevelt stands behind a podium as he tells the American people that Japan has attacked the United States at Pearl Harbor and the country is at war. Annapolis Naval Historical Wax Museum. CENTER: Britain's wartime leader Winston Churchill. Churchill's fingers are raised in his famous "V for Victory" sign. *Courtesy Wax Museum at Fisherman's Wharf* RIGHT: Churchill *(right)* is seated near Field Marshal Bernard Montgomery, who commanded the British Eighth Army in North Africa and, later, the British armies that invaded France. Royal London Wax Museum (Victoria).

BOTTOM: Montgomery *(right)* and Churchill *(seated)* appear with General De Gaulle at Potter's Wax Museum.

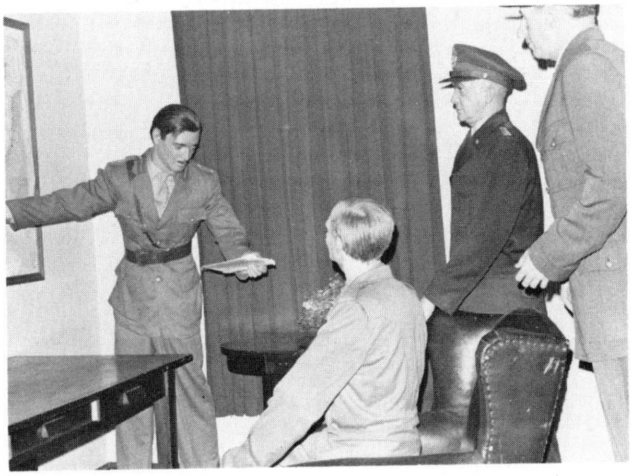

TOP, LEFT: Among the World War II figures at the Royal London Wax Museum (Victoria) is Lord Louis Mountbatten, Supreme Allied Commander in Southeast Asia. RIGHT: At Louis Tussaud's English Wax Museum (Niagara Falls) distinguished figures from the World War II years include *(from left)* Field Marshal Montgomery, Premier Joseph Stalin, General Charles de Gaulle, and General Dwight D. Eisenhower.

CENTER: The London Wax Museum of Boston hangs a noose between Adolf Hitler *(left)* and Hideki Tojo. Hitler committed suicide a few days before Germany's defeat. In 1946 Tojo was tried as a war criminal, found guilty, and executed.

BOTTOM, LEFT: General Dwight D. Eisenhower, Commander of Allied Forces in Europe, here receives a briefing on the weather expected in Normandy on June 6, 1944, the day of the Allied invasion of France. National Historical Wax Museum. RIGHT: General Eisenhower. Hall of American Presidents Wax Museum.

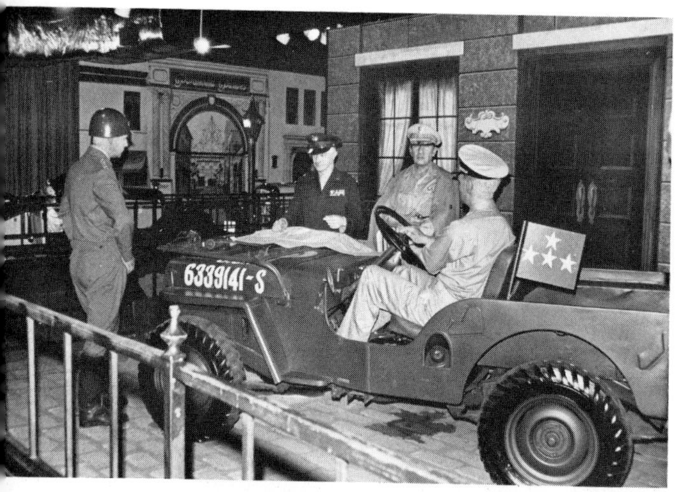

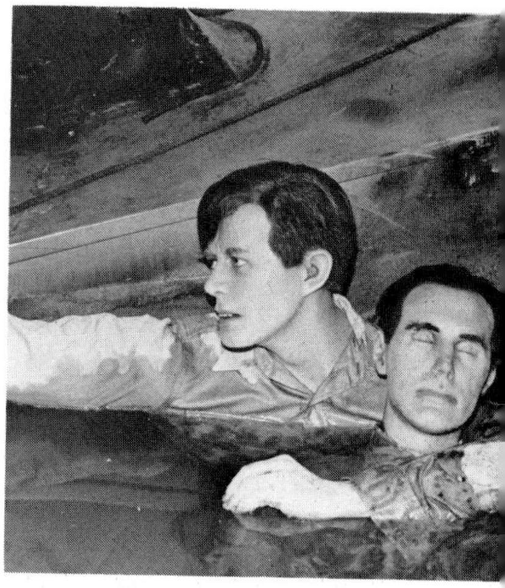

TOP, LEFT *(from left):* Generals George S. Patton, Dwight D. Eisenhower, and Douglas MacArthur around a World War II jeep at Houston's Classic Showcase. Admiral Chester Nimitz sits behind the steering wheel. CENTER: This likeness honors naval hero Admiral William Halsey. During World War II Halsey commanded U.S. forces in the South Pacific. *Courtesy Annapolis Naval Historical Wax Museum* RIGHT: A close-up of John F. Kennedy and one of the men he rescued after the future president's torpedo boat had been sliced in two by a Japanese destroyer. London Wax Museum of Boston.

CENTER, LEFT: Lieutenant John F. Kennedy carves a message on a coconut, requesting help. Friendly natives delivered the message to a naval base and the PT-109 survivors were rescued. *Courtesy Miami Wax Museum.* RIGHT: The Yalta Conference at which plans were made for the postwar world. The conference, held in February 1945, was attended by *(from left)* the Soviet Union's Joseph Stalin, President Franklin D. Roosevelt of the United States, and British Prime Minister Winston Churchill. *Courtesy Shrine to Democracy Wax Museum*

BOTTOM: The surrender ceremony aboard the U.S.S. *Missouri* that ended World War II. The figures represent *(from left)* Admiral Chester Nimitz, General Douglas MacArthur, Japanese Foreign Minister Mamoru Shigemitsu, and a representative of the Japanese Imperial General Staff. *Courtesy Annapolis Naval Historical Wax Museum*

3 PRESIDENTS AND THEIR FIRST LADIES

Although the presidents of the United States have been of unequal stature, all have played a role in their country's history, a fact that is reflected in the many representations of presidents on display in wax museums. The presidents appear singly and in groups; often they are posed in tableaux illustrating important events of their administrations.

Also represented in a number of wax museums are the nation's First Ladies. In addition to presiding over the White House, many First Ladies have made distinctive contributions to their husbands' administrations.

By studying the lifelike wax portraits of our Chief Executives and their First Ladies—and reading the informative material provided about each—one can come away with a greater appreciation of the presidency and the men and women who have occupied the White House.

LEFT: Martha Washington, the nation's first First Lady, presided over "White Houses" in New York City and Philadelphia. During those years she was described as white-haired, rather short, plump, and neat in appearance. Here she is dressed in the mobcap and flowing gown of the period. Hall of Presidents Wax Museum.

BELOW: When George Washington married Martha Custis on January 6, 1759, the bride wore a yellow silk dress. Martha's children, Jack and Patsy, appear with the couple in a re-creation of the wedding which took place in the drawing room of Martha's country home near Williamsburg. Williamsburg National Wax Museum.

TOP, LEFT: The re-creation of a tea party attended by President and Mrs. Washington on July 1, 1791. Their hosts were Lancaster County's General Edward Hand *(standing)* and his wife *(right). Courtesy National Wax Museum of Lancaster County Heritage* RIGHT *(from left):* John Adams, George Washington, Thomas Jefferson, and Benjamin Franklin. *Courtesy Miami Wax Museum*

CENTER, LEFT: Lafayette, the French nobleman who fought for the American cause during the Revolution *(far left)* is visiting the Washingtons at Mount Vernon in this tableau at the National Historical Wax Museum. The figure representing Martha Washington is seated at right. The visit took place in 1784. RIGHT: A close-up of Lafayette's visit to Mount Vernon. Miami Wax Museum.

BOTTOM, LEFT: This tableau re-creates Lafayette's visit to Lancaster. *Courtesy National Museum of Lancaster County Heritage* RIGHT: John Adams, the second president of the United States *(right)* as he may have appeared when he traveled to France with Benjamin Franklin *(left)* to negotiate peace terms with Great Britain at the end of the Revolutionary War. After several diplomatic missions Adams served as Washington's vice-president (1788-96) before assuming the presidency in 1797. Adams was the first president to occupy the White House, then still unfinished.

TOP, LEFT: John Adams at the Hall of American Presidents Wax Museum in Chattanooga. CENTER: Thomas Jefferson sits at a table similar to the one he used in Philadelphia during the summer of 1776 when he was writing the Declaration of Independence. Jefferson became the third president of the United States in 1800 in a contest decided by the House of Representatives after a tie electoral vote between Jefferson and Aaron Burr. Jefferson served two terms in the White House. Hall of Presidents Wax Museum. RIGHT: The famous duel between Aaron Burr, Thomas Jefferson's vice-president, and Alexander Hamilton. Hamilton, fatally wounded, lies on the ground supported by a friend. The victorious Burr stands at right. National Historical Wax Museum.

CENTER, LEFT: For five years Thomas Jefferson stuided law with George Wythe, a Williamsburg lawyer. Figures of Jefferson and his teacher can be seen at the Williamsburg National Wax Museum. RIGHT: James Madison, fourth president of the United States at the Hall of American Presidents Wax Museum in Chattanooga.

BOTTOM: A re-creation of Dolley Madison's drawing room in the Executive Annex, the house at Pennsylvania Avenue and 19th Street in Washington occupied by the Madisons while the burned White House was being rebuilt. Here, Dolley Madison is chatting with John Quincy Adams who was to become the sixth president of the United States. Hall of Presidents Wax Museum.

TOP, LEFT: At the other end of the Madison drawing room, a uniformed figure, General Andrew Jackson, who was to become the seventh president of the United States, shakes hands with Secretary of State James Monroe, who was elected to the presidency in 1816 and 1820, and is best remembered for his Monroe Doctrine warning against attempts by European powers to establish colonies in America. President James Madison is descending the staircase at the right. Dolley Madison is standing at the extreme left. The seated figure is Rachel Jackson. RIGHT: The sixth president of the United States, John Quincy Adams. Hall of Presidents in Gettysburg.

CENTER, LEFT: Rachel and Andrew Jackson in a garden setting. During her husband's campaign for the presidency, Rachel Jackson, a divorcée, was the subject of malicious gossip concerning her remarriage. She died shortly before Jackson was elected in 1828. *Courtesy Shrine to Democracy Wax Museum* CENTER: Here, President Martin Van Buren, a widower for eighteen years when he moved into the White House, poses with his daughter-in-law Angelica, who acted as his hostess. Hall of Presidents Wax Museum.
RIGHT: Models of President Van Buren and Angelica appear in a setting that suggests a Washington reception during Van Buren's term of office. The president is at Angelica's right. At her left are Senator Daniel Webster of Massachusetts; former President John Quincy Adams, then serving in the House of Representatives; and Senator John Calhoun of South Carolina. *Courtesy Shrine to Democracy Wax Museum*

BOTTOM: President of the United States for just one month before he succumbed to pneumonia, William Henry Harrison, at sixty-eight, was the oldest man ever to be elected to that office. The ninth president can be seen at the Colorado Springs Hall of Presidents Wax Museum.

TOP, LEFT: The first vice-president of the United States to succeed to office on the death of a president, John Tyler soon lost the support of his party, the Whigs, and was formally read out of its membership. When his term of office ended in 1845, Tyler withdrew from politics and returned to his Virginia plantation. The tenth president appears to be delivering a speech. Hall of Presidents Wax Museum. CENTER: Brought forward at the Democratic convention in 1844 to break a deadlock between two other candidates for the presidential nomination, James Polk went on to win the nomination and the election. This representation of the eleventh president is at the Hall of Presidents Wax Museum. RIGHT: A popular figure at the Hall of American Presidents Wax Museum is that of David Rice Atchison, who as president pro tempore of the Senate was technically the president of the United States for one day on Sunday, March 4, 1849. President Zachary Taylor was inaugurated on Monday, March 5, 1849.

CENTER, LEFT: Zachary Taylor *(right)*, who died in 1850 after only fifteen months in office, appears with his successor, Millard Fillmore. Gettysburg's Hall of Presidents. RIGHT: Three one-term presidents *(from left)*: Millard Fillmore, Franklin Pierce, and James Buchanan. During their administrations, which spanned the years 1850 to 1861, the controversy between the North and the South that eventually resulted in the Civil War eroded the presidents' standing with the party. Hall of Presidents Wax Museum.

BOTTOM: James Buchanan, the fifteenth president of the United States and our only bachelor president, appears on the doorstep of his Pennsylvania home. Buchanan's niece, Harriet Lane, who served as his White House hostess, stands at the president's side. *Courtesy National Wax Museum of Lancaster County Heritage*

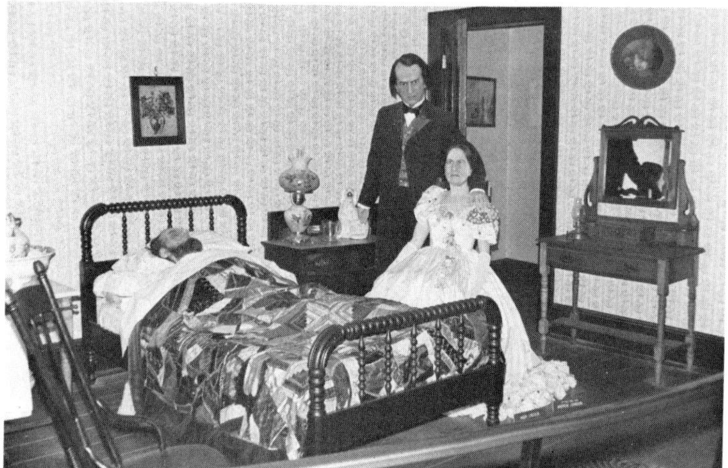

TOP, LEFT: This close-up of the upper portion of Abraham Lincoln's wax effigy shows the attention to detail that went into its preparation. *Courtesy Miami Wax Museum* RIGHT: Lincoln's debates with Stephen A. Douglas in 1858, when both men were seeking election to the Senate, gave Lincoln national prominence although he lost the election. Douglas favored allowing the states to decide if they wanted to abolish slavery. A beardless figure of Lincoln appears to be making a point during a debate. The president grew a beard between his election and his inauguration. *Courtesy Shrine to Democracy Wax Museum*

CENTER: President Lincoln's assassination at Ford's Theater on the night of April 14, 1865. Mrs. Lincoln is seated at the president's right. Behind them, gun in hand, is a figure representing John Wilkes Booth, the actor who killed Lincoln in an attempt to avenge the South. Josephine Tussaud Wax Museum.

BOTTOM: Abraham Lincoln's death in the lodging house across the street from Ford's Theater where he was carried after being shot. The president died with members of his family and government officials at his bedside. Hall of Presidents Wax Museum *(left)* and the Burning Springs Wax Museum.

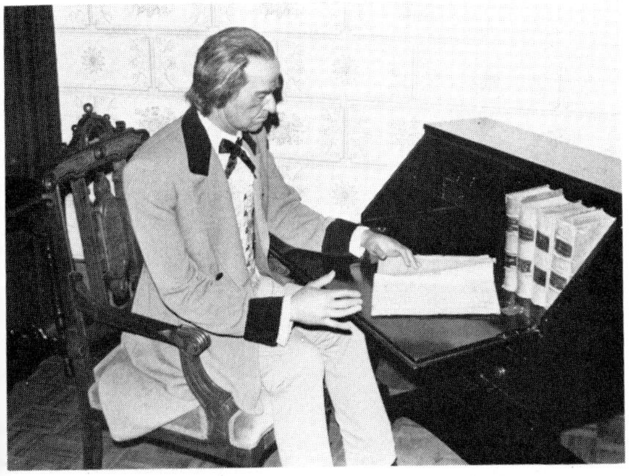

TOP, LEFT: Andrew Johnson, who succeeded to the presidency upon Lincoln's death. In 1868 difficulties between Johnson and Secretary of War Edwin M. Stanton led to an attempt to impeach the president which failed by one vote. American Historical Wax Museum. CENTER: Victorious Civil War General Ulysses S. Grant, who became the eighteenth president of the United States, proved less adept as a politician than as a military commander. His appointees were involved in several major scandals and his administration was unable to prevent the economic collapse that began in 1873. RIGHT: President Rutherford B. Hayes became the country's nineteenth president only after a bitterly disputed election had been decided by a special commission (when the Republican party failed to nominate Hayes for a second term, he retired to his native Ohio). While Hayes was president, the inventor Thomas Edison visited the White House to demonstrate his phonograph, re-created here. The president is listening to the newly installed White House telephone. *Courtesy Shrine to Democracy Wax Museum*

CENTER, LEFT: Charles Guiteau *(left)* has just fired two bullets at President James Garfield. The shooting took place at a railway station in Washington on July 2, 1881. All attempts to save the life of the twentieth president failed and he died on September 19, 1881. Hall of Presidents Wax Museum. RIGHT: Chester Arthur, who became president upon Garfield's death, at the Hall of American Presidents Wax Museum. Arthur was a widower with two children when he became president.

BOTTOM: In 1886 Grover Cleveland, then forty-nine, married twenty-one-year-old Frances Folsom in a small White House ceremony, reproduced here. President of the United States from 1885 to 1889 and from 1893 to 1897, he was the only man to serve two nonconsecutive terms in the White House and the only chief executive to be married there. Hall of Presidents Wax Museum.

TOP, LEFT: Benjamin Harrison, the last of the Civil War generals to become president, held that office between Grover Cleveland's two terms. Harrison was the grandson of William Henry Harrison, the ninth president of the United States. While Harrison was in the White House, Congress passed, and the president signed, the McKinley Tariff Act designed to protect American industry from foreign imports. Here President Harrison *(left)* stands with the author of the tariff bill, William McKinley. In 1897 McKinley became the twenty-fifth president of the United States. Hall of Presidents Wax Museum. CENTER: Noted financial and industrial tycoons of the 1890s in a setting that suggests they may have been invited to the White House by President Benjamin Harrison. They are *(from left)* John Pierpont Morgan, John D. Rockefeller, and Andrew Carnegie. Hall of Presidents Wax Museum. RIGHT: William McKinley, the third president of the United States to be assassinated within a period of thirty-six years, assumed office in 1897. The Spanish-American War took place during his second year in the White House. Hollywood Wax Museum.

CENTER, LEFT: When President McKinley was shot while visiting Buffalo, New York, in September, 1901, Vice-President Theodore Roosevelt was notified by telegram. This is a re-creation of the Adirondack Mountains railway station platform where a vacationing Roosevelt received the news. Louis Tussaud's English Wax Museum (Atlantic City). RIGHT: An older Theodore Roosevelt in the ex-president's trophy room of his house in Oyster Bay, New York, to which he retired in 1909. After leaving the presidency, Roosevelt and his twenty-two-year-old son, Kermit, went on a lengthy African hunting trip. *Courtesy Shrine to Democracy Wax Museum*

BOTTOM: Theodore Roosevelt's contemporaries *(left to right):* Henry Ford, Thomas Edison, and prizefighter John L. Sullivan. Mammoth Cave Wax Museum.

TOP, LEFT: William Howard Taft, whose portly figure is on display here, served his country both as president (1909-13) and chief justice of the Supreme Court (1921-30). The six-foot-two-inch Taft weighed over three hundred pounds. Hall of Presidents Wax Museum. CENTER: The three presidential candidates in the 1912 election *(from left):* Woodrow Wilson, the Democratic candidate who won the election; Republican William Howard Taft, who failed in his reelection attempt; and Theodore Roosevelt, who also lost as the candidate of the Progressive, or "Bull Moose" party. National Historical Wax Museum. RIGHT: Woodrow Wilson, the twenty-eighth president of the United States as he appeared at the Versailles Conference at the end of World War I. During his postwar campaign to win approval for the Treaty of Versailles, Wilson suffered a disabling stroke. He made a partial recovery and finished his term of office. Before he became president, Wilson was governor of New Jersey and before that president of Princeton University. *Courtesy Shrine to Democracy Wax Museum*

CENTER, LEFT: Supposedly picked as a presidential candidate in 1920 because he "looked like a president," Warren Harding presided over an administration that became engulfed in scandal. Harding, who was not personally involved in any malfeasance, died before completing his term as twenty-ninth president. Hall of Presidents Wax Museum in Colorado Springs. RIGHT: President Calvin Coolidge's swearing-in ceremony. The rite took place at 2:30 A.M. on August 3, 1923, at Plymouth Notch, Vermont, where Coolidge was visiting his father when President Harding died. The elder Coolidge, a notary public, administered the oath of office. The frugal, quiet Coolidge was a popular president, but in 1928 he announced that he "did not choose to run" again. He retired to Massachusetts where he died in 1933. National Historical Wax Museum.

BOTTOM: Mining-engineer-turned-politican Herbert Hoover had the misfortune to become president just as the Great Depression of 1929 was about to begin. His proposals for restoring prosperity were not effective and he was not reelected in 1932. Hall of Presidents Wax Museum.

TOP, LEFT: In his inaugural speech on March 4, 1933, Franklin Delano Roosevelt told his depression-ridden countrymen: "The only thing we have to fear is fear itself." Here is a re-creation of the scene with wax figures of *(from left):* Chief Justice Charles Evans Hughes, outgoing President Herbert Hoover, the new president, and Eleanor Roosevelt. National Historical Wax Museum. RIGHT: President Roosevelt seated in a swing. The thirty-second president's legs were paralyzed following an attack of poliomyelitis in 1921, when he was thirty-nine, and he was unable to stand or walk without help. Underground Wax Museum.

BOTTOM, LEFT: The first of several wartime conferences between American President Franklin D. Roosevelt, the only man to be elected to that office four times, and British Prime Minister Winston Churchill began at the White House on December 22, 1941. On Christmas Eve the two leaders delivered a joint radio message. Figures are Roosevelt *(left)* and Churchill before radio microphones. Eleanor Roosevelt stands at right. In noticeably deteriorating health during his 1944 campaign for reelection, Roosevelt died on April 12, 1945, at Warm Springs, Georgia, where he had gone for a rest. Hall of Presidents Wax Museum. CENTER: President Roosevelt *(right)* posed with Harry S Truman, who succeeded him as president of the United States. Josephine Tussaud Wax Museum of the *Queen Mary.*
RIGHT: Anna Eleanor Roosevelt, First Lady longer than anyone in United States history, and the most active of all presidential wives. During her years in the White House she traveled thousands of miles visiting Americans at home and overseas, and wrote, lectured, and assisted with countless projects. *Courtesy Wax Museum at Fisherman's Wharf*

TOP, LEFT: Truman liked to play the piano, and the National Historical Wax Museum has accommodated the thirty-third president. Some of the determination that Harry S Truman displayed during his years in the White House has been captured here. Upon becoming president in 1945, Truman had to face such problems as the use of the first atomic bomb, demobilization of American Armed Forces, conversion to a peacetime economy, and the containment of communism. Although many of his decisions were unpopular, he was returned to office by an upset victory in the 1948 elections. CENTER: World War II hero Dwight David Eisenhower won a landslide victory in the 1952 elections. Moreover, he managed to retain his widespread popularity during his eight years in office. This figure of the thirty-fourth president is on display at Madame Tussaud's in London. RIGHT: President Eisenhower with his Secretary of State, John Foster Dulles. Miami Wax Museum.

BOTTOM, LEFT: President John F. Kennedy in a setting based on his inauguration in 1961. In his inaugural address Kennedy called for a global alliance against "tyranny, poverty, disease, and war itself." Wax Museum at Denver. RIGHT: The upper portion of a John F. Kennedy figure as part of a tableau depicting a 1962 meeting at the White House between President Kennedy and Golda Meir, then the Israeli Minister of Foreign Affairs. *Courtesy Shalom Palace Wax Museum*

TOP, LEFT: Senator Edward Kennedy *(center)* with brother Robert and the president. Josephine Tussaud Wax Museum. RIGHT: Former First Lady Jacqueline Kennedy. Mammoth Cave Wax Museum.

CENTER, LEFT: A re-creation of the arrival of President and Mrs. John F. Kennedy *(left)* and Texas Governor and Mrs. John B. Connally at Love Field in Dallas, Texas, on November 22, 1963. While the president was being driven into Dallas in an open car, he was assassinated by Harvey Lee Oswald. Governor Connally was severely wounded. *Courtesy Southwest Historical Wax Museum* RIGHT: Along with its wax figures and other exhibits, the Movie Wax Museum at Estes Park displays a diorama that shows President Kennedy's motorcade at the moment the fatal shots were fired from a building housing the Texas School Book Depository.

BOTTOM: Some of the many world leaders who gathered in Washington for President Kennedy's funeral. Grouped around a replica of the eternal flame at the graveside are *(from left)* Emperor Haile Selassie of Ethiopia; Robert Kennedy; John Kennedy, Jr.; Jacqueline Kennedy; Martin Luther King, Jr.; Caroline Kennedy; H.R.H. Prince Philip, the husband of the Queen of England; and Charles de Gaulle, president of France. Hall of Presidents Wax Museum.

TOP, LEFT: Lyndon Johnson succeeded to the presidency after a long and distinguished career in politics that included service in both the House of Representatives and the Senate. This figure of the thirty-sixth president appears at the Wax Museum in Denver. RIGHT: A close look at a wax portrait of Lyndon Johnson shows how skillfully the sculptor has reproduced the former president's features. *Courtesy Wax Museum at Fisherman's Wharf*

CENTER, LEFT: Richard Nixon, who became the thirty-seventh president of the United States in 1969, is posed with First Lady Pat Nixon. Hall of Presidents Wax Museum. CENTER: Richard Nixon holds a reel of tape similar to those used in the secret White House taping system. The tapes implicated the president and closest aides in an attempt to thwart an investigation into a break-in at the Democratic party headquarters in Washington. On August 9, 1974, under threat of impeachment, Richard Nixon resigned from the presidency. Louis Tussaud's English Wax Museum (Niagara Falls). RIGHT: Gerald R. Ford, the thirty-eighth president of the United States. When he assumed the presidency in 1974 after Richard Nixon resigned, Ford became the first president to occupy that office without being chosen in a national election. Earlier, he had been named to the vice-presidency when Spiro T. Agnew resigned under pressure of indictment for wrongdoing. Royal London Wax Museum in Phoenix.

BOTTOM: Madame Tussaud's wax figure of President Jimmy Carter in the Grand Hall. *Courtesy Madame Tussaud's (London)*

The Smithsonian Institution's First Ladies

In the Smithsonian Institution's First Ladies Hall, the nation's First Ladies are represented by an impressive array of mannequins. The mannequins are not wax figures, however. At one time the Smithsonian's First Ladies were made of plaster of Paris, but now polyester resin is used. While no attempt has been made to reproduce an exact likeness of a First Lady's face, the expression of the eyes, hair style, skin tone, and size of the figure resemble as closely as possible written descriptions, photographs, paintings, and other representations of the individual First Ladies.

Some of the First Ladies in the Smithsonian's collection were not presidential wives, but relatives or friends who, for various reasons, performed the duties of official White House hostess.

Garbed in authentic dresses from the Institution's collection, the Smithsonian's First Ladies are displayed in period room settings which feature design details of actual White House rooms and furnishings owned and used by presidential families.

An overall view of the Smithsonian Institution's First Ladies Hall.

TOP, LEFT: Abigail Adams holds a sequin-spangled fan that actually belonged to Mrs. Adams. CENTER: Martha Jefferson Randolph served as a hostess for her father, Thomas Jefferson, who had been a widower for eighteen years when he became president. RIGHT: Mary Todd Lincoln *(left)* is one of several First Ladies gracing a replica of a White House parlor decorated in the Victorian style. In the background: Jane Pierce *(left)* and Abigail Fillmore.

CENTER, LEFT: Seen in another view of the Victorian parlor are *(from left)* Mary Todd Lincoln, Martha Johnson Patterson (daughter of President Andrew Johnson), and Harriet Lane. RIGHT: The First Ladies of five administrations are represented in the corner of the replica of the White House East Room seen here. *From Left:* Florence Kling Harding, Grace Goodhue Coolidge, Lou Henry Hoover, Anna Eleanor Roosevelt, and Bess Wallace Truman.

BOTTOM: Mannequins representing *(from left)* Mamie Eisenhower, Jacqueline Kennedy, and Lady Bird Johnson stand in another part of the East Room replica in the First Ladies Hall.

The Hall of First Ladies at Gettysburg's Hall of Presidents

At the Hall of Presidents in Gettysburg, Pennsylvania, a special exhibit is devoted to "petite-sized" representations of the First Ladies. The figures in the Hall of First Ladies at Gettysburg are made of porcelain. Their hair styles are copied from those the First Ladies wore when they attended their husbands' inaugural ceremonies and their dresses are authentic reproductions of gowns that were part of each First Lady's wardrobe.

LEFT: Abigail Adams *(right)* and Martha Jefferson Randolph, President Thomas Jefferson's daughter and official hostess. Abigail Adams, the wife of President John Adams, was the first First Lady to preside over the White House. She is the only First Lady to also become the mother of a president. Her son, John Quincy Adams, was the sixth president of the United States. CENTER: First Lady Elizabeth Monroe as she appears at the Hall. Mrs. Monroe was famous for her beauty. RIGHT: John Tyler became the first president of the United States to be married in office when he took Julia Gardiner as his bride in 1844.

4 LEADERS— AMERICANS AND OTHERS WHO INFLUENCED AMERICAN LIFE

In planning its exhibits, a wax museum chooses from among many potential candidates. In the case of men and women who have achieved positions of leadership, the choice is wide, covering historical as well as modern times and many fields of endeavor. Whatever the basis for selection—contributions the individual has made toward a better world, his or her presence in the history books used by millions of Americans, general popularity, status as a native son or daughter who made good—a wax museum's representations of national and world leaders give one a chance to meet the famous face to face and to become better acquainted with those who have helped shape the course of our history.

RIGHT: Native son Senator Barry Goldwater is honored here. Goldwater, who was elected to the Senate from Arizona in 1952, was an unsuccessful candidate for the presidency in 1964. Royal London Wax Museum in Phoenix.

FAR RIGHT: Movie-actor-turned-politician Ronald Reagan, a leader of the conservative wing of the Republican party, was Governor of California from 1966 to 1974. Josephine Tussaud Wax Museum of the *Queen Mary*.

TOP, LEFT: Venerable Texas politician Sam Rayburn. Rayburn, a longtime member of the House of Representatives from Texas, was Speaker of the House during ten sessions of Congress. Southwestern Historical Wax Museum. RIGHT: Huey Long, controversial governor of Louisiana (1928-31) and United States senator from that state (1931-35), appears in a characteristic speaking pose at the Musée Conti. In 1935 Long was assassinated by the son of a political opponent.

BOTTOM: Three famous justices of the Supreme Court *(from left):* Earl Warren, who served as chief justice from 1953 to 1969; Oliver Wendell Holmes, an associate justice from 1902 until 1935; and John Marshall, who as chief justice from 1801 until 1835, established the principle of judicial review. National Historical Wax Museum.

TOP, LEFT: Civil rights leader Dr. Martin Luther King, Jr. The black leader launched the civil rights movement in 1955 when he was a young Baptist minister in Montgomery, Alabama. *Courtesy Wax Museum at Fisherman's Wharf* RIGHT: Dr. King is posed as if he were addressing an audience. A gifted speaker and a champion of nonviolence in the civil rights movement, King was awarded the Nobel Peace Prize in 1964. He was assassinated in 1968. Pioneer Square Wax Museum.

BOTTOM, LEFT: Dr. Ralph Bunche, the distinguished American who served as under-secretary of the United Nations and who received the Nobel Peace Pize in 1950. National Historical Wax Museum. RIGHT: Pioneer black educator Booker T. Washington, seen here, is among the noted Americans represented at the Miami Wax Museum. Washington, the founder and longtime head of Tuskegee Institute in Tuskegee, Alabama, devoted his life to the cause of black education.

TOP, LEFT: A close-up of Leonid Brezhnev from an exhibit called "World of Renown" at Atlanta's Underground Wax Museum—a rotating glass globe that encircles wax portraits of the world's leaders. RIGHT: Indian Prime Minister Indira Gandhi as she appears in the "World of Renown" exhibit.

CENTER, LEFT: Pierre Elliott Trudeau, who became prime minister of Canada in 1968. Madame Tussaud's in London. SECOND FROM LEFT: Chairman Mao *(left)* appears with Leonid Brezhnev, first secretary of the Communist Party of the Soviet Union. Madame Tussaud's in London. SECOND FROM RIGHT: Generalissimo Chiang Kai-shek, head of the Nationalist Chinese government on Taiwan until his death in 1975. Potter's Wax Museum. RIGHT: Revolutionary patriot José Martí represents a dramatic period in Cuba's colonial history. From his exile in the United States, Marti kept alive the hope of Cuban independence from Spain.

BOTTOM, LEFT: Cuban revolutionary leader and Premier Fidel Castro in battle garb. London Wax Museum of Boston. RIGHT: This close-up of Castro shows the skill of the wax sculptor. *Courtesy Wax Museum at Fisherman's Wharf*

TOP: Two former Chancellors of the Federal Republic of Germany appear together: *(left)* Willy Brandt, who held the office from 1969 to 1974, and *(right)* Konrad Adenauer, chancellor from 1949 to 1963. Madame Tussaud's in London.

CENTER, LEFT: British statesman Winston Churchill posed with a 1938 Rolls-Royce. Churchill served as Britain's prime minister from 1940 to 1945 and from 1951 to 1955. In 1963 he was made an honorary citizen of the United States, the first person living outside the United States to receive that honor. Classic Showcase in Houston. RIGHT: Churchill before an easel. Painting was one of his hobbies. He was also an amateur bricklayer and a prolific author. Louis Tussaud's English Wax Museum (Niagara Falls).

BOTTOM, LEFT: Pipe-smoking British Prime Minister Harold Wilson. Wilson, who served as Labor prime minister from 1964 to 1970, was returned to office in 1974. Louis Tussaud's English Wax Museum (Niagara Falls). RIGHT: Edward Heath, seen here, was Britain's prime minister from 1970 to 1974. Royal London Wax Museum (Victoria).

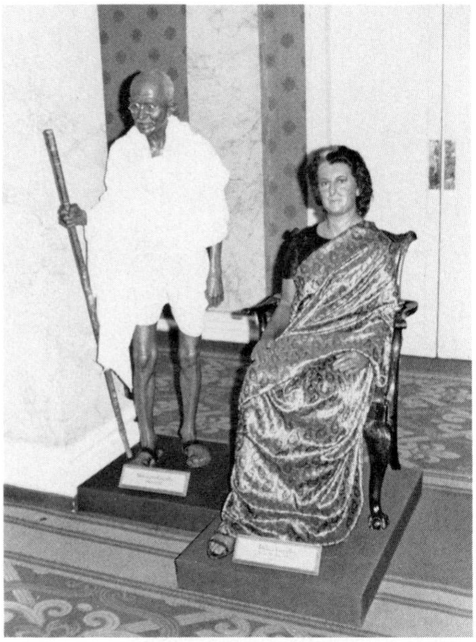

TOP, LEFT: Details of a carefully crafted Mahatma Gandhi head. *Courtesy Wax Museum at Fisherman's Wharf* RIGHT: Mahatma Gandhi next to Indira Gandhi, who became prime minister of India in 1966. No relation to Mahatma Gandhi, Indira Gandhi was the daughter of former Indian Prime Minister Jawaharlal Nehru. Madame Tussaud's in London.

CENTER, LEFT: Golda Meir, premier of Israel from 1969 until her resignation in 1974. She grew up in Milwaukee, Wisconsin, and taught school there before migrating to Palestine in 1921. Louis Tussaud's English Wax Museum (Atlantic City). CENTER: Israel's first Prime Minister, David Ben-Gurion, who helped found the State of Israel. Louis Tussaud's English Wax Museum (Atlantic City). RIGHT: A close-up of the upper portion of Nikita S. Khrushchev, first secretary of the Soviet Union's Communist Party and—from 1958 until he was retired in 1964—premier. He died in 1971. *Courtesy Wax Museum at Fisherman's Wharf*

BOTTOM: Nikita Khrushchev *(center)*, Mao Tse-tung *(left)*, and Fidel Castro make a happy trio. London Wax Museum of Boston.

TOP, LEFT: Alexander Solzhenitsyn at Madame Tussaud's in Amsterdam. In 1974 the Nobel Prize-winning author and outspoken critic of the Soviet system was exiled from the Soviet Union. He now lives in Vermont. CENTER: President of Yugoslavia Marshal Tito's wax likeness was surreptitiously removed from its museum in 1965 and deposited at the door of the Yugoslav Embassy in London. Madame Tussaud's in London. RIGHT: Pope Paul VI at the Wharf Wax Museum. Paul VI became head of the Roman Catholic Church in 1963.

BOTTOM, LEFT: Napoleon Bonaparte, called the outstanding military genius of modern times. His battlefield victories made him the national hero of France and in 1803 he was crowned Emperor Napoleon, a title he retained until he was exiled after losing the Battle of Waterloo in 1815. Louis Tussaud's English Wax Museum (Atlantic City). RIGHT: Napoleon greets visitors to the Josephine Tussaud Wax Museum's Hall of Battles.

DISTINGUISHED AMERICANS 5

Through the medium of wax it is possible to become better acquainted with men and women who have made unique contributions to life in America. The choice of subjects available to museums is wide, ranging from individuals of local interest to persons of national importance, but all have made worthwhile contributions.

ABOVE: George Washington Carver. Among the many accomplishments of the distinguished black scientist, botanist, and educator was the development of new uses for peanuts and other agricultural products. Southwestern Historical Wax Museum. RIGHT, TOP: At Houston's Classic Showcase Carver *(left)* appears with automobile manufacturer Henry Ford. BELOW: George Washington Carver *(left)*, Henry Ford *(center)*, and inventor Thomas A. Edison. One of Edison's inventions, the phonograph, is displayed with the trio. American Historical Wax Museum.

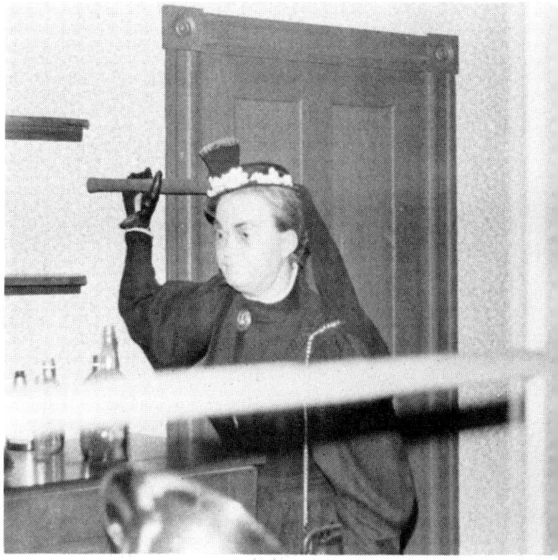

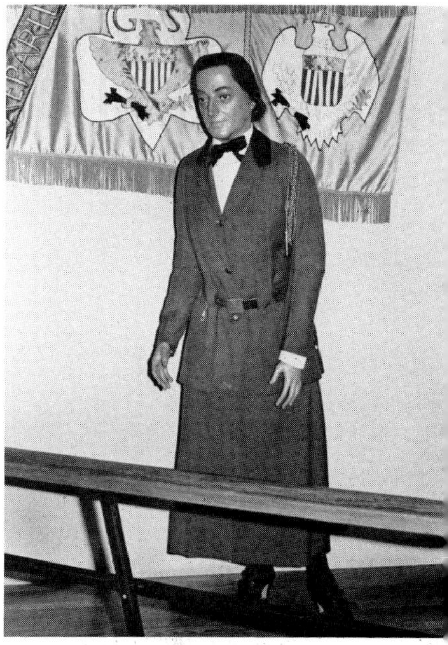

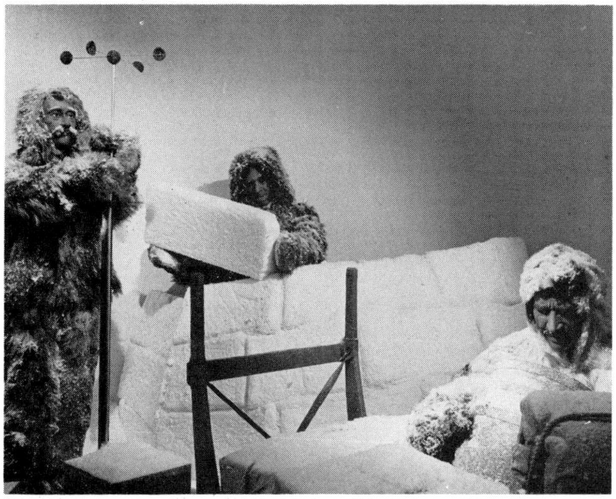

TOP, LEFT: Thomas A. Edison *(right)* is seen here with the noted physicist Albert Einstein. *Courtesy Tokyo Tower Wax Museum* CENTER: Albert Einstein at the Royal Pacific Wax Museum at Newport, Oregon. RIGHT: Carry Nation in a decidedly militant pose. The reformer carried out a forty-two-year campaign against alcohol, tobacco, and other vices. National Historical Wax Museum.

CENTER, LEFT: The founder of the Boy Scouts in the United States, Daniel Carter Beard *(right, facing camera),* has been posed as if he were being painted by artist Norman Rockwell. National Historical Wax Museum. RIGHT: Juliette Gordon Low, the founder of the Girl Scouts. National Historical Wax Museum.

BOTTOM: Admiral Robert Peary's journey to the North Pole, which he reached on April 6, 1909, is the subject of this tableau. He is on the left. *Courtesy Annapolis Naval Historical Wax Museum*

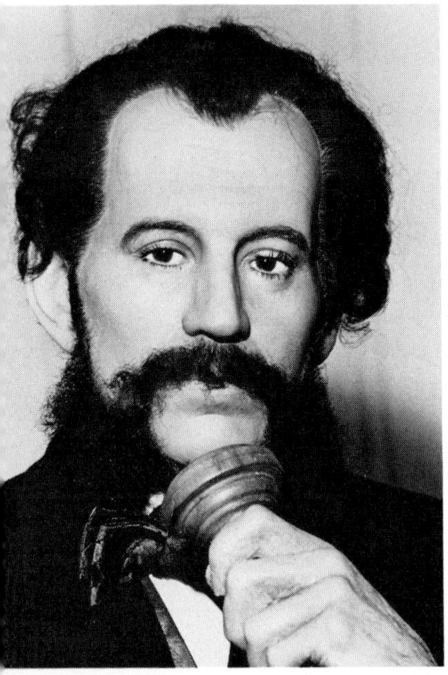

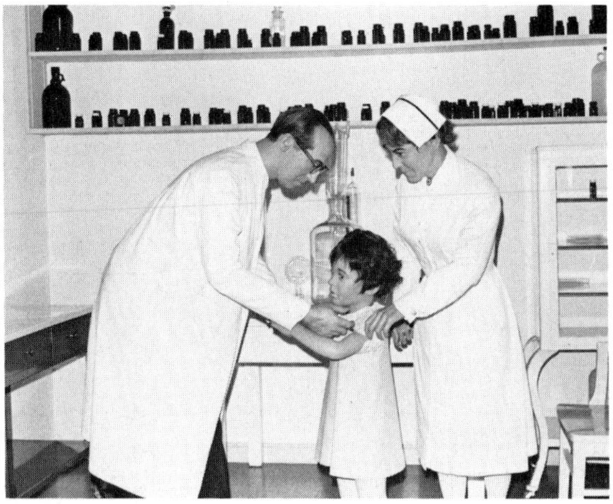

TOP, LEFT: Head of Alexander Graham Bell's portrait. Bell, a scientist and teacher of the deaf, patented the telephone in 1876. *Courtesy Shrine to Democracy Wax Museum* CENTER: Bell with Helen Keller who, born blind and deaf, used some of the techniques developed by him in learning to communicate. Burning Springs Wax Museum. RIGHT: Leaders of industry and labor are represented by this group. *From left:* oilmen Edwin F. Drake and John D. Rockefeller *(seated),* labor leader Samuel Gompers, and steel manufacturer and philanthropist Andrew Carnegie. National Historical Wax Museum.

CENTER: Two pioneers in the field of medicine. *Left:* Dr. William Thomas Morton, the Boston dentist who was the first to use anesthesia on a patient. *Right:* Dr. Jonas Salk, who developed a vaccine that is almost wholly effective against polio.

BOTTOM: At the Southwestern Historical Wax Museum Van Cliburn sits at a piano. Cliburn became a prominent concert pianist after winning a piano competition in Moscow in 1958.

TOP, LEFT: Writers Nathaniel Hawthorne *(left)* and Washington Irving share a cozy corner at Potter's Wax Museum. RIGHT: Novelist Owen Wister *(left)*, best known for ***The Virginian***, as he appears at Denver's Wax Museum, and poet and short story writer Edgar Allan Poe at the London Wax Museum of Boston.

BOTTOM, LEFT: Novelist Jack London whose more than forty books include the popular *The Call of the Wild, The Sea Wolf,* and *Martin Eden,* was a native of San Francisco. Wharf Wax Museum. CENTER: This close-up of writer Ernest Hemingway shows how amazingly lifelike wax figures can be. *Courtesy Wax Museum at Fisherman's Wharf* RIGHT: Novelist Zane Grey's likeness is made of plaster, rather than wax. The figure wears clothes that belonged to Grey and sits in a room that is a replica of one in which he did much of his writing. *Courtesy National Road—Zane Grey Museum*

TOP, LEFT: Two museums, San Francisco's Chinatown Wax Museum and Seattle's Pioneer Square Wax Museum, tell the story of Chinese immigrants and their contribution to the United States. The Chinatown Wax Museum is devoted entirely to scenes depicting San Francisco's Chinatown as it once was and to important events in Chinese history. Seen here is a diorama at the Chinatown museum featuring two workers chipping away rock during the building of the Central Pacific Railroad. They have been lowered down the mountain face in baskets. During the 1860s Chinese immigrants played an important part in the building of the Central Pacific and other railroads. *Courtesy Chinatown Wax Museum* RIGHT: In Seattle, Oriental laborers who had come to the United States to help build the railroads faced opposition when they began to take other jobs as the railroads neared completion. This diorama depicts the attempt by a Seattle mob, in 1886, to force Chinese to leave the city. Pioneer Square Wax Museum.

CENTER, LEFT: Because many of San Francisco's early Chinese settlers worked in laundries, the museum presents a typical Chinese laundry scene. *Courtesy Chinatown Wax Museum* RIGHT: An herb shop similar to those in which San Francisco's Chinese residents purchased traditional remedies for their ailments has been re-created. The man wearing a hat *(right)* is undergoing a "pulse diagnosis" administered by an herb doctor. *Courtesy Chinatown Wax Museum*

BOTTOM, LEFT: Tongs, the fraternal organizations that played an important role in Chinese society, were transplanted to the United States by Chinese immigrants. This group represents a tong initiation rite. *Courtesy Chinatown Wax Museum* RIGHT: Hiram Leong Fong, the first American of Chinese descent to be elected to the United States Senate. Fong, a resident of Hawaii, was elected to the Senate from that state in 1959 and reelected in 1964 and 1970. National Historical Wax Museum.

6 ROYAL EFFIGIES

Royalty has always had a fascination for Americans. Even at the time of the War for Independence, the protests of the colonists were aimed more at the arbitrary use of the taxing power than at the institution of monarchy. More recently, American-born Princess Grace of Monaco has been accorded the status of a national heroine, and articles about the comings and goings of the world's kings, queens, princes, and princesses have a wide audience among American magazine and newspaper readers. Therefore, it is not surprising that royal effigies, often dressed in regal robes and jeweled crowns, are among the most popular of wax museum exhibits.

The wax portraits of the British royal family seen here are the most popular exhibits in Madame Tussaud's Grand Hall. *From left:* Mark Phillips, husband of Princess Anne; Princess Anne; Prince Charles; Queen Elizabeth II; her husband, Prince Philip, Duke of Edinburgh; and the Queen Mother.

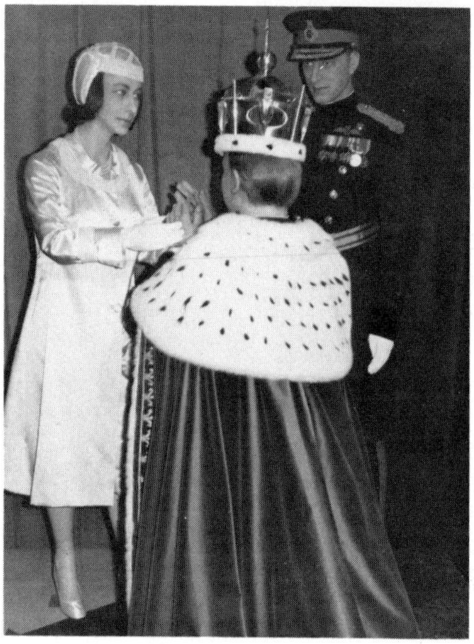

TOP, LEFT: Queen Elizabeth II in coronation robes and Prince Philip in a naval officer's uniform. Wax Museum at Fisherman's Wharf. RIGHT: Elizabeth looks on while Philip *(on right)* greets his uncle (and the Queen's cousin), Lord Louis Mountbatten. All three are descendants of Queen Victoria. Josephine Tussaud Wax Museum of the *Queen Mary.*

CENTER, LEFT: The investiture of Prince Charles, son of Queen Elizabeth II and Prince Philip, as Prince of Wales. The original ceremony took place in 1969 at Caernarvon Castle in Wales. *From left:* the Queen, Prince Charles, and Prince Philip. Royal London Wax Museum at Phoenix. RIGHT: The Duke and Duchess of Windsor. As King Edward VIII, the Duke of Windsor occupied the British throne for eleven months before abdicating in 1936 to marry "the woman I love," American divorcée Wallis Warfield Simpson. Musée Conti.

BOTTOM: The Duke of Windsor *(second from left)* appears with his brother, King George VI *(left);* his mother, Queen Mary; his father, King George V. Madame Tussaud's in London.

TOP, LEFT: King George V and Queen Mary. George V occupied the English throne from 1910 until his death in 1936. Josephine Tussaud Wax Museum of the *Queen Mary.* RIGHT: Portraits of Britain's King George VI and Queen Elizabeth, parents of Queen Elizabeth II. Josephine Tussaud Wax Museum of the *Queen Mary.*

CENTER: Henry VIII of England is surrounded by authentically costumed likenesses of his six wives. *Courtesy Underground Wax Museum*

BOTTOM, LEFT: Henry VIII. Louis Tussaud's English Wax Museum (Niagara Falls). RIGHT: Catherine of Aragon, Henry VIII's first wife and queen for more than twenty years. Louis Tussaud's English Wax Museum (Niagara Falls).

TOP, LEFT: George III, who was king of England at the time of the American Revolution. Louis Tussaud's English Wax Museum (Niagara Falls). RIGHT: During her sixty-four-year reign, Queen Victoria presided over the worldwide expansion of the British Empire. The indomitable sovereign seen here is on display at Louis Tussaud's English Wax Museum (Niagara Falls).

CENTER: These scenes featuring Louis XV illustrate the elegance of mid-eighteenth-century French court life. *Left:* Louis XV with Madame Du Barry at Louis Tussaud's English Wax Museum (Niagara Falls). *Right:* Louis XV with Madame de Pompadour at Louis Tussaud's English Wax Museum (Atlantic City).

BOTTOM, LEFT: Prussian King Frederick II, known as Frederick the Great because of his victories on the battlefield. Potter's Wax Museum. RIGHT: Haile Selassie, Emperor of Ethiopia from 1930 until he was deposed in 1974. He died the following year. Madame Tussaud's in London.

TOP, LEFT: Wax portrait of Prince Rainier and Princess Grace of Monaco is a popular attraction. *Courtesy Wax Museum at Fisherman's Wharf* RIGHT: Rulers who have affected the course of history *(from left):* Catherine the Great, Julius Caesar, Cleopatra, Queen Victoria *(seated),* Alexander the Great, Henry VIII, and Napoleon. *Courtesy London Wax Museum in St. Petersburg*

CENTER, LEFT: Cleopatra, mistress of Julius Caesar and Mark Antony, in a courtyard setting with the two famous Romans. Louis Tussaud's English Wax Museum (Niagara Falls). RIGHT: Cleopatra greets Julius Caesar *(at right)* after being smuggled into his presence rolled up in a carpet. Louis Tussaud's English Wax Museum (Atlantic City).

BOTTOM: Cleopatra in her bath. Royal London Wax Museum in Phoenix.

SPACEMEN AND AVIATORS 7

Those twentieth-century pioneers, the men who left the surface of the earth, first in airplanes and then in spacecraft, are represented in wax museums, especially those involved in that crowning achievement of the United States space program, the first manned landing on the moon. Here we see a space-suit-clad Astronaut Neil Armstrong take man's first step on the moon. Moreover, we can get a better view of the astronaut and the surrounding moonscape than was available on television and can study the re-creation of that historic event as long as we wish.

We can see wax portraits of the Wright brothers when they worked on the first successful airplane, and can study the accurately reproduced features of the twenty-five-year-old Charles Lindbergh, the first man to make a solo transatlantic flight.

Armstrong, the Wright brothers, and Lindbergh are but a few of the figures from the fascinating world of aviation and space flight on display.

RIGHT: Moonwalker Neil Armstrong. *Courtesy Shalom Palace Wax Museum*

BELOW: Apollo 11 Astronauts Neil Armstrong and Edwin E. Aldrin who visited the moon are seen at Madame Tussaud's in London.

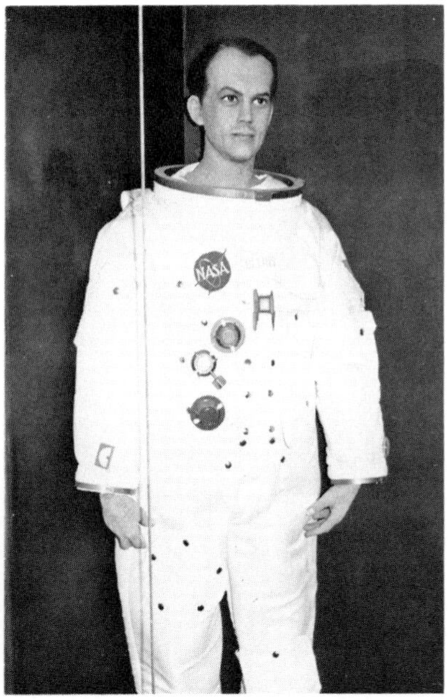

TOP, LEFT: Astronaut Michael Collins, the third member of the Apollo 11 crew, who traveled around the moon in the Apollo 11 command module while Astronauts Armstrong and Aldrin explored the lunar surface. Royal London Wax Museum (Victoria). CENTER: Astronaut Aldrin can be viewed through a window that looks out on a replica of the area in the moon's Sea of Tranquility, where he landed. Royal London Wax Museum (Victoria). RIGHT: "We feel great. We feel just perfect," astronauts *(from left)* Aldrin, Collins, and Armstrong assure President Richard Nixon on July 25, 1969, after their safe return from the moon. The astronauts are seen through a reproduction of the window of their special quarantine station aboard the carrier U.S.S. *Hornet. Courtesy Shrine to Democracy Wax Museum*

BOTTOM, LEFT: The bicycle shop where Orville and Wilbur Wright are working on their wooden wind tunnel. National Historical Wax Museum. CENTER: This likeness of Charles A. Lindbergh, who, in 1927 at the age of twenty-five, electrified the world by making the first solo, nonstop flight from New York to Paris, is on display at the Burning Springs Wax Museum. RIGHT: An airplane propeller serves as a backdrop for Amelia Earhart, one of the first professional women fliers. She made a solo, nonstop Atlantic flight in 1932, and in 1937 disappeared during a flight over the Pacific. Hollywood Wax Museum.

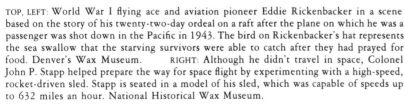

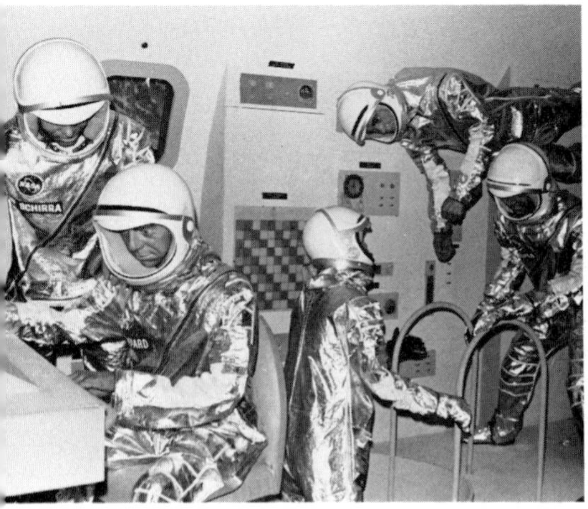

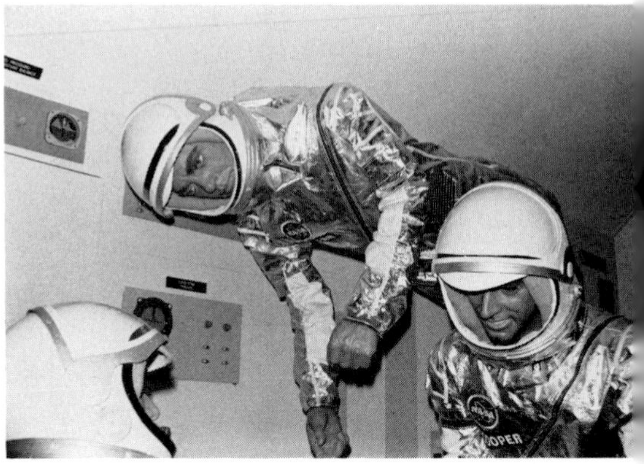

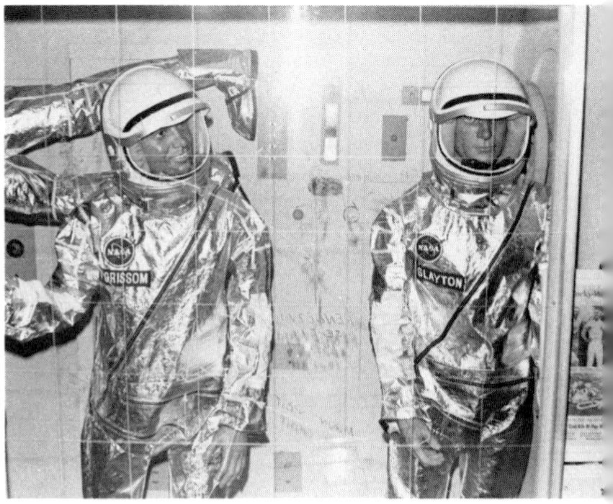

TOP, LEFT: World War I flying ace and aviation pioneer Eddie Rickenbacker in a scene based on the story of his twenty-two-day ordeal on a raft after the plane on which he was a passenger was shot down in the Pacific in 1943. The bird on Rickenbacker's hat represents the sea swallow that the starving survivors were able to catch after they had prayed for food. Denver's Wax Museum. RIGHT: Although he didn't travel in space, Colonel John P. Stapp helped prepare the way for space flight by experimenting with a high-speed, rocket-driven sled. Stapp is seated in a model of his sled, which was capable of speeds up to 632 miles an hour. National Historical Wax Museum.

CENTER, LEFT: The Denver Wax Museum has constructed the interior of a spaceship for its display of the first American astronauts. *From left:* Walter M. Shirra, Alan B. Shepard, Jr., M. Scott Carpenter, L. Gordon Cooper, and John H. Glenn, Jr. *(floating in a horizontal position).* CENTER: Astronaut Shepard, the first American to travel in space (in 1961), commanded the Apollo 14 moon mission in 1971. *Courtesy Annapolis Naval Historical Wax Museum* RIGHT: In the Denver re-creation, John Glenn appears to be floating near the ceiling of a gravity-free spaceship. In 1962 Glenn became the first American to orbit the earth.

BOTTOM: Astronauts Virgil I. Grissom *(left)* and Donald K. Slayton in the Denver museum's spaceship. Grissom, who made successful flights in the Mercury and Gemini space projects, was killed in a fire aboard the Apollo 1 spacecraft in 1967. Slayton commanded the American team in a joint Soviet Union–United States space mission in 1975.

8 FAMOUS SPORTS FIGURES AND EVENTS

Most of the wax museums throughout the world have figures depicting sports heroes and heroines or a famous sports event in history. Here are the sports greats, from Jim Thorpe to Hank Aaron, from Jack Dempsey to Muhammed Ali, including golf's Ben Hogan, Olympic star Mark Spitz, and jockey Eddie Arcaro, and even Sir Edmund Hillary, the first man to reach the top of Mount Everest.

ABOVE: O. J. Simpson in 1968 while a running back for the University of Southern California. In 1973, with the Buffalo Bills, Orenthal James Simpson set a pro football season's rushing record of 2,003 yards. Louis Tussaud's English Wax Museum (Niagara Falls).

RIGHT: Byron "Whizzer" White, a star back at the University of Colorado in 1935-37, played pro football for the Pittsburgh Steelers and the Detroit Lions and then, in 1962, the Rhodes Scholar was appointed a justice of the U.S. Supreme Court. Wax Museum at Denver.

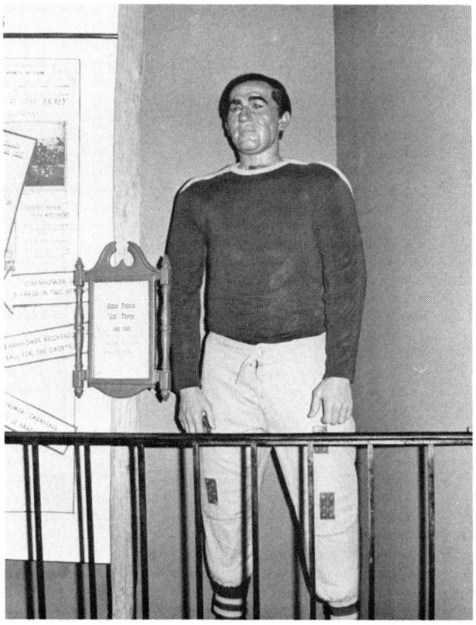

TOP, LEFT: Probably the most famous player-coach in American football history, Knute Rockne spent his life with Notre Dame University. As coach, he amassed a record 105 wins, 12 losses, and 5 ties before being killed in an airplane accident in 1931. Potter's Wax Museum. CENTER: Jim Thorpe, from tiny Carlisle College (Pennsylvania) for Indians, was known as the perfect athlete. At the Olympic Games in Stockholm in 1912 he swept the pentathlon, winning all five events, then, the decathlon, including the javelin. But Thorpe played semipro ball in 1911, so he was stripped of his gold medals. National Historical Wax Museum. RIGHT: Lou Gehrig had a fourteen-year career as a New York Yankee. The record book is open. He never batted below .300 in twelve years. He played 2,130 consecutive games, a record which no one has ever equaled. Pioneer Square Wax Museum.

BOTTOM, LEFT: Jackie Robinson, the gutty Dodger who helped inspire the image that this nation was capable of racial understanding. He paved the way for the black athlete, and when he retired in 1956 black athletes were streaming into all sports. The famous Brooklyn Dodger is seen coming up to bat. American Historical Wax Museum. RIGHT: Babe Ruth, the King of Swat, America's most famous baseball player. For most of his career he played for the New York Yankees. When his career ended in 1935 he had accumulated a record total of 714 home runs. Mammoth Cave Wax Museum.

TOP, LEFT: Ruth *(seated)* with Hank Aaron who in 1974 broke the Babe's record of 714 lifetime home runs. Aaron holds the National League lifetime record for "runs batted in"—more than 2,000.

CENTER: Willie Mays, star batter, base runner, and fielder, considered the best all-around baseball player in his time. Nicknamed the "Say Hey Kid." Wax Museum at Fisherman's Wharf. RIGHT: Mickey Mantle of the New York Yankees, considered one of the fastest men in baseball before he retired due to injuries. Mantle hit .300 or more in each of five seasons (1954-58), along with 38 home runs or more and over 100 r.b.i.'s each season. He was voted Most Valuable Player in the American League for three of these five years. Southwestern Historical Wax Museum.

BOTTOM, LEFT: Joe DiMaggio. "Joltin' Joe" was known as the "Yankee Clipper" because of his smooth playing style as an outfielder for thirteen years with the New York Yankees. In 1941 he established a record that is still intact—batting safely in fifty-six consecutive games. He was also a onetime husband of Marilyn Monroe. Wax Museum at Fisherman's Wharf. RIGHT: Casey Stengel, the greatest American baseball manager, achieved wide acclaim as the leader of the New York Yankees, capturing ten American League championships and seven world championships in the twelve seasons he led them (1949–60). His death in 1975 stirred the baseball world. Musée Conti.

TOP, LEFT: The "most dramatic boxing scene in history." John L. Sullivan is shown rising from the floor after being knocked out in the twenty-first round of his world championship fight with contender James J. Corbett in 1892. Sullivan, never before defeated, was reported to have said at that moment, "What happened?" When told that Corbett had knocked him out, he replied, "Is that all that happened to me? I thought I'd fallen off the Brooklyn Bridge." Musée Conti. RIGHT: The Dempsey-Willard fight. Jack Dempsey, twenty-four years of age, KO'd Jess Willard, thirty-seven, in the third round of their bout on July 4, 1919, in Toledo, Ohio. He held the heavyweight crown from 1919 until 1926. The Wax Museum, Denver.

BOTTOM, LEFT: Dempsey in a ring. National Historical Wax Museum. CENTER: Max Baer. In 1934 he defeated the giant Primo Carnera at Madison Square Garden, knocking him off his feet eleven times in the fight, to become the world champion for exactly one year until James Braddock beat him in fifteen rounds. Wax Museum at Fisherman's Wharf. RIGHT: Joe Louis, known as the "Brown Bomber," became the heavyweight champion in 1937, when he defeated James Braddock in eight rounds at Chicago. He held the crown twelve years, more than any champion in the history of boxing. Wax Museum at Fisherman's Wharf.

TOP, LEFT: Ben Hogan, one of the top professional golfers in the United States. He was U.S. Professional Golfers Association Champion in 1946 and 1948. This is the figure of him in the Wax Museum in Boston. CENTER: Mildred (Babe) Didrikson Zaharias, the Texan named woman athlete of the year five times by the Associated Press. The Press also voted her the greatest female athlete of the first half of the twentieth century. *Courtesy Southwestern Historical Wax Museum* RIGHT: Mark Spitz in the Atlantic City wax museum. He won a record seven gold medals for swimming in the Munich Olympics in 1972.

BOTTOM, LEFT: Eddie Arcaro, even after years of retirement, is still considered the greatest jockey in the United States. He rode the great and famous Citation for Calumet Farm. National Historical Wax Museum. CENTER: Nancy Greene, Canadian Alpine ski racer, and the first woman to win the World Ski Cup. She won an Olympic gold medal in the giant slalom at Grenoble in 1968. Mammoth Cave Wax Museum. RIGHT: Sir Edmund Hillary *(right)* and his native guide, Sherpa Tenzing, reaching the top of Mount Everest in this scene in the Victoria Wax Museum. On May 29, 1953, Hillary and his guide became the first two men in history to set foot on the summit of this 29,002-foot mountain, the highest in the world.

LAND OF STORYBOOKS 9

Storybook characters, loved by generations of children, have been modeled by the same wax sculptors who fashion likenesses of the world's famous men and women. Displayed in wax museums in scenes based on the stories in which they appear, Alice, Red Riding Hood, Cinderella, Pinocchio, Long John Silver, and a host of others bring back fond memories for young and old.

From *Snow White and the Seven Dwarfs. From left:* Dwarfs Dopey and Sleepy at the Josephine Tussaud Wax Museum and Sneezy at the Royal London Wax Museum in Phoenix.

TOP, LEFT: *Grimm's Fairy Tales* characters Hansel and Gretel, with the witch's house at right. Underground Wax Museum. RIGHT: The Victoria Royal London Wax Museum's version of the witch in *Hansel and Gretel.* Her house is at left.

CENTER, LEFT: Red Riding Hood and the infamous wolf star in this scene. *Courtesy Wax Museum at Fisherman's Wharf* RIGHT: When this photo was taken a museum worker was adjusting Red Riding Hood's hair. Royal London Wax Museum in Victoria.

BOTTOM: Little Jack Horner has a corner all to himself at the Wax Museum at Fisherman's Wharf.

TOP, LEFT: Prince Charming is about to rescue Sleeping Beauty, who has been asleep for a hundred years as a result of a spell cast by the wicked fairy Carabosse. *Courtesy Wax Museum at Fisherman's Wharf.* CENTER: Winnie-the-Pooh, who enlivens A. A. Milne's *Winnie-the-Pooh* and *The House at Pooh Corner,* waits to greet young readers at the Royal London Wax Museum (Phoenix.). RIGHT: Cinderella as she looked after her transformation. Wax Museum at Fisherman's Wharf.

BOTTOM, LEFT: Josephine Tussaud Wax Museum's Cinderella with a pumpkin coach. RIGHT: In this scene based on the Arthurian legend, King Arthur *(standing at right)* is knighting Sir Lancelot. Queen Guinevere is at left. Royal London Wax Museum (Niagara Falls).

TOP, LEFT: Peter Pan, the little boy in J. M. Barrie's play who ran away to Never-Never-Land and never grew up. Royal London Wax Museum (Victoria). RIGHT: Peter Pan *(right)* appears with the scheming Captain Hook whom Peter manages to outwit in the play. Hall of Presidents Wax Museum.

BOTTOM, LEFT: Washington Irving's humorous character Rip Van Winkle, who slept for twenty years, shares exhibit space with a dwarf. Wharf Wax Museum. CENTER: Hans Christian Andersen, the Danish writer whose fairy tales have been read by generations of children. Madame Tussaud's in London. RIGHT: Lewis Carroll's immortal Alice. Wax Museum at Fisherman's Wharf.

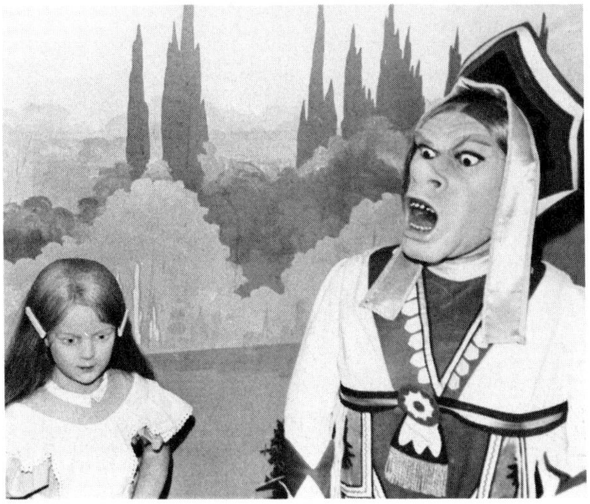

TOP, LEFT: Two of the odd characters that Alice met in Wonderland, the cook *(left)* and the Duchess (holding the baby who turned into a pig). Wax Museum at Fisherman's Wharf. RIGHT: Alice encounters the King and Queen of Hearts. *Courtesy London Wax Museum (St. Petersburg Beach)*

CENTER, LEFT: Alice with the Queen of Hearts. London Wax Museum of Boston. RIGHT: The famous Mad Hatter's tea party in *Alice in Wonderland. Courtesy Royal London Wax Museum (Chicago)*

BOTTOM: Uncle Remus, the storyteller created by Joel Chandler Harris, is at the Underground Wax Museum.

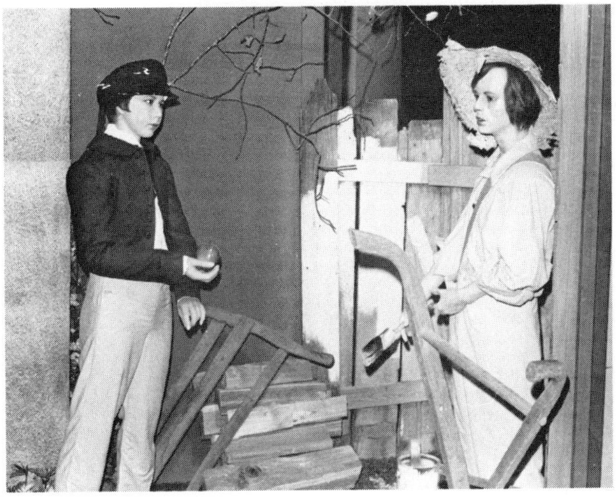

TOP, LEFT: Joel Chandler Harris, author of the Uncle Remus stories. Underground Wax Museum. RIGHT: Jack climbing the beanstalk from the giant's castle. He carries the goose that laid the golden egg. London Wax Museum of Boston.

CENTER: Based on Henry Wadsworth Longfellow's poem "The Wreck of the Hesperus," the captain's daughter is seen in a tableau at the London Wax Museum of Boston.

BOTTOM: Episodes from Mark Twain's ever-popular *The Adventures of Tom Sawyer* are portrayed at the Underground Wax Museum *(left)* and the London Wax Museum of Boston.

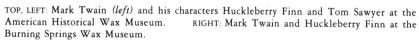

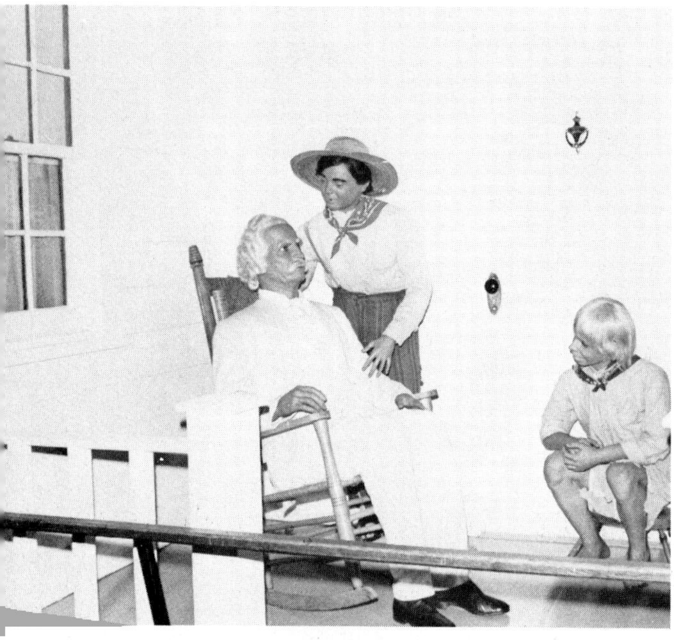

TOP, LEFT: Mark Twain *(left)* and his characters Huckleberry Finn and Tom Sawyer at the American Historical Wax Museum. RIGHT: Mark Twain and Huckleberry Finn at the Burning Springs Wax Museum.

BOTTOM, LEFT: Close-ups of Geppetto *(left)* and Pinocchio. London Wax Museum of Boston.

BOTTOM, RIGHT: Robert Louis Stevenson, author of *Treasure Island,* one of the most popular adventure books ever written for young people. Potter's Wax Museum.

TOP, LEFT: Long John Silver, the pirate leader from *Treasure Island. Courtesy Wax Museum at Fisherman's Wharf* CENTER: This saucy gentleman is one of more than a hundred merry buccaneers in the "Pirates of the Caribbean" attraction at Disneyland. His winking salute is to boat-borne visitors (not seen) below. The red-nosed mate is celebrating the looting and burning of a port city on the Spanish Main where he and many other "Audio-Animatronics" all over Disneyland and Walt Disney World have been keeping visitors entertained. *Courtesy Walt Disney Productions* RIGHT: The miser Ebenezer Scrooge, one of the characters in Dickens's beloved *Christmas Carol,* in a scene in which he is counting his money. The ghost of his dead partner Marley lights up in the background. Louis Tussaud's English Wax Museum (Atlantic City).

BOTTOM, LEFT: Walt Disney with a sketchbook. Mammoth Cave Wax Museum. CENTER: Disney posed as though he were telling a story to a young fan. Josephine Tussaud Wax Museum of the *Queen Mary.* RIGHT: The Audio-Animatronics system at Disneyland includes two of eighteen lifelike comical bears from the exhibit "Country Bear Jamboree": Henry *(left),* the show's "bearitoned" master of ceremonies, and Gomer, his honey-lovin' sidekick who plays the honky-tonk piano. Walt Disney World has a similar "Country Bear Jamboree." *Courtesy Walt Disney Productions*

CHAMBER OF HORRORS 10

Following a tradition established by Madame Tussaud, most wax museums include a "Chamber of Horrors" among their exhibits. Here, representations of notorious criminals of the past and present share space with famous monsters of fiction. Some Chamber of Horrors figures are about to perpetuate an evil deed; others are fascinating in their horridness. Also included among the macabre exhibits are various instruments of torture, once actually used to punish the guilty or those unfortunate enough to be considered guilty.

Boris Karloff was the classic Frankenstein's monster in the movies. He often commented that nursery tales such as Hansel and Gretel had more horror in them than Frankenstein movies and that horror movies had their basis in children's stories.

At the Boris Karloff Wax Museum in Niagara Falls, Canada, their literature states, "Mr. Karloff was particularly concerned with the small fry, since a large portion of his fan mail was from children. When asked about the effect of his horror films on children, Mr. Karloff quoted many a bloodthirsty line from nursery tales, most of them well known to our children and told by loving parents at bedtime. We would like you to know Mr. Karloff's opinion of this type of horror: 'Horror is a misnomer for it means revulsion. Terror, which is a much better word, is to make people's hair stand on end, not to make them lose their breakfast.' "

Master of mystery and suspense Alfred Hitchcock welcomes visitors to the Chamber of Horrors. Josephine Tussaud Wax Museum.

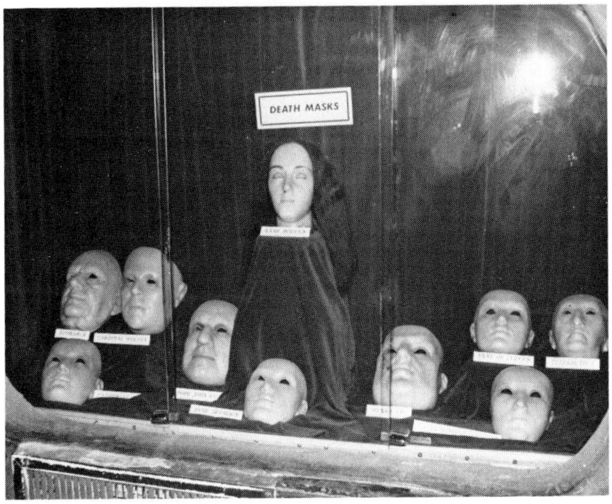

TOP: A likeness of Boris Karloff, the "King of Terror," greets visitors. Boris Karloff Wax Museum.

CENTER: One of Madame Tussaud's most popular exhibits was the working model of a guillotine which she displayed in her "Separate Room." Instruments for beheading continue to fascinate wax museum visitors. Seen here are the guillotines on display at *(left)* Louis Tussaud's English Wax Museum (Atlantic City) and the Hollywood Wax Museum.

BOTTOM: Reproductions of the death masks of famous persons in the Chamber of Horrors. Louis Tussaud's English Wax Museum (Niagara Falls).

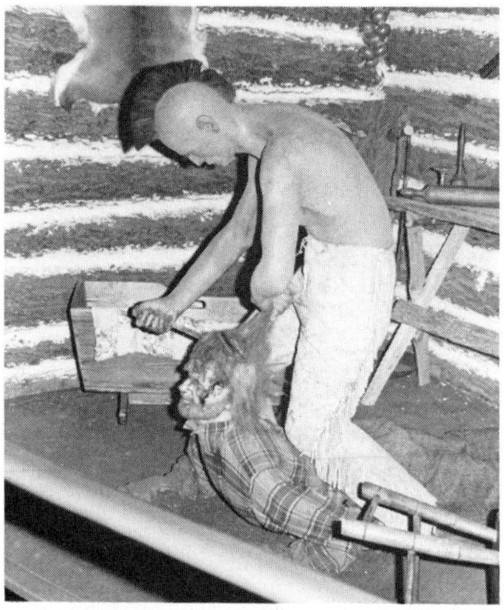

TOP AND CENTER: Gruesome scenes from the Chamber of Horrors *(from top):* the ritual sacrifice of an Aztec youth; an example of punishment by whipping, as practiced in colonial America; and a scalping. Louis Tussaud's English Wax Museum (Atlantic City).

BOTTOM: These incarnations of Count Dracula, the vampire of legend, fiction, and film fame, await visitors to the Musée Conti and the Underground Wax Museum.

TOP, LEFT: Quasimodo, the deformed bellringer in Victor Hugo's *The Hunchback of Notre Dame.* Musée Conti *(left)* and the Hollywood Wax Museum. RIGHT: Scary indeed is this representation, based on a movie, of a mummy who came back to life. *Courtesy Wax Museum at Fisherman's Wharf*

CENTER AND LEFT: The monster created by Dr. Frankenstein in Mary Shelley's novel is a popular wax museum subject. These versions of the loathsome creature can be seen at the Wax Museum at Fisherman's Wharf, the Musée Conti, and the Royal London Wax Museum (Chicago). *Courtesy Wax Museum at Fisherman's Wharf* and the *Royal London Wax Museum (Chicago)*

House of Frankenstein Wax Museums at Lake George in New York State and Niagara Falls in Canada cater to Chamber of Horror fans. Seen here is a selection of their exhibits.

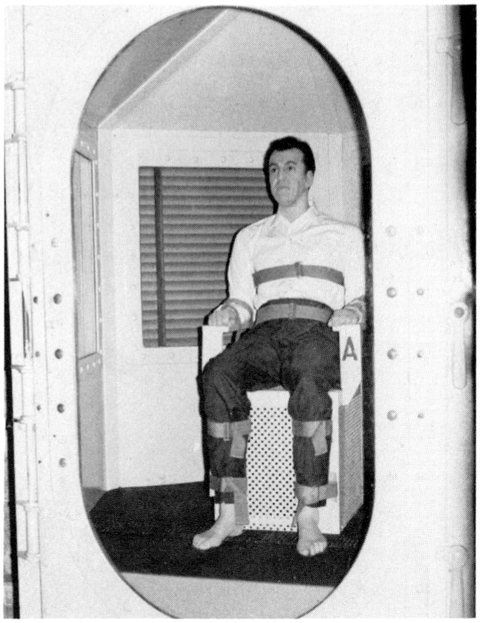

TOP, LEFT: According to legend, a werewolf is a person capable of assuming the form of a wolf. London Wax Museum of Boston. CENTER AND RIGHT: These Chamber of Horrors denizens were photographed at the Boris Karloff Wax Museum. *From left:* Satan and a witch.

CENTER, LEFT: Two real-life masters of evil: Adolf Hitler, Germany's World War II leader *(left),* and Adolf Eichmann, responsible for the death of millions of Jews. Royal London Wax Museum (Victoria). RIGHT: Caryl Chessman, the American who was finally executed in 1960 after spending twelve years in the death row of a California prison, appears in an electric chair at Madame Tussaud's.

BOTTOM: A re-creation of the gory end, in 1891, of an attempt by organized crime to control New Orleans. Outraged citizens, taking justice into their own hands, are shooting members of the gang charged with assassinating the New Orleans chief of police. Musée Conti.

TOP, LEFT: Notorious bank robber John Dillinger, shot by FBI agents in Chicago in 1934. Louis Tussaud's English Wax Museum (Niagara Falls). RIGHT: Gangster Al Capone *(left)* and friends appear in a tableau set in a Prohibition era speakeasy. *Courtesy Tokyo Tower Wax Museum*

CENTER: Al Capone *(seated at rear)* posed with *(from left)* gangsters Johnny Torrio, Jack McGurn, and Bugs Moran. *Courtesy London Wax Museum*

BOTTOM: A smiling Al Capone appears with a "moll." *Courtesy Royal London Wax Museum in Chicago (left),* and at the Josephine Tussaud Wax Museum.

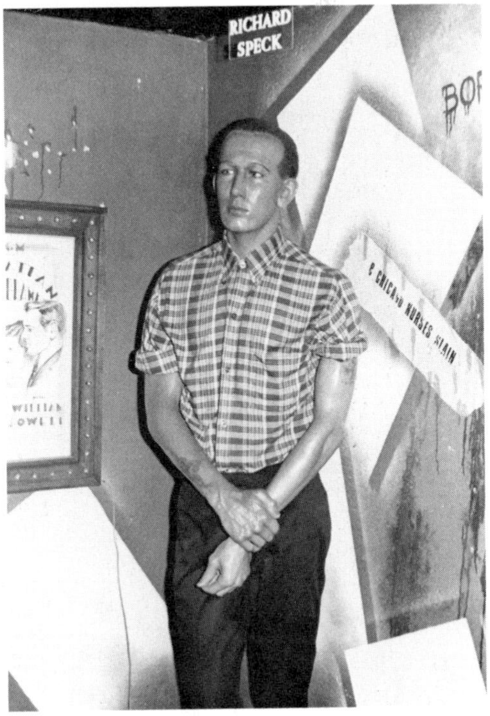

TOP: A Southwestern Historical Wax Museum photograph displays these likenesses of Bonnie Parker and Clyde Barrow whose criminal exploits supplied the story lines for the move *Bonnie and Clyde.* Faye Dunaway as she appears in the role of Bonnie Parker at the Royal Pacific Wax Museum at Newport, Oregon.

BOTTOM: Mass killers *(from left)* Charles Manson, *courtesy of the Shalom Palace Wax Museum;* and Charles Whitman and Richard Speck, at Louis Tussaud's English Wax Museum in Niagara Falls.

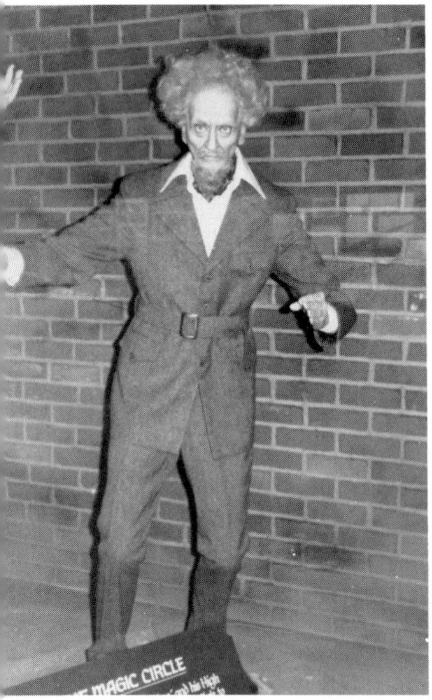

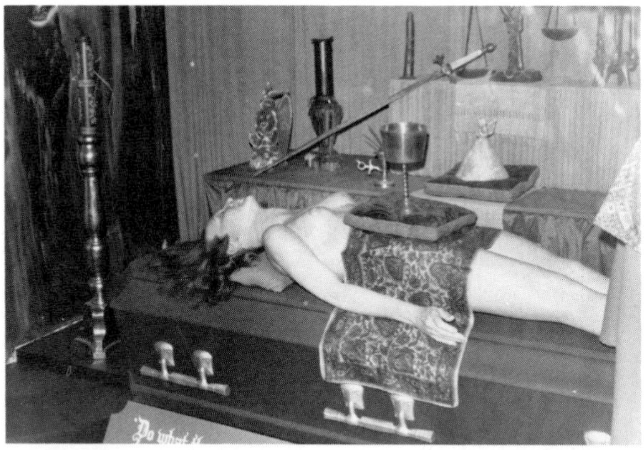

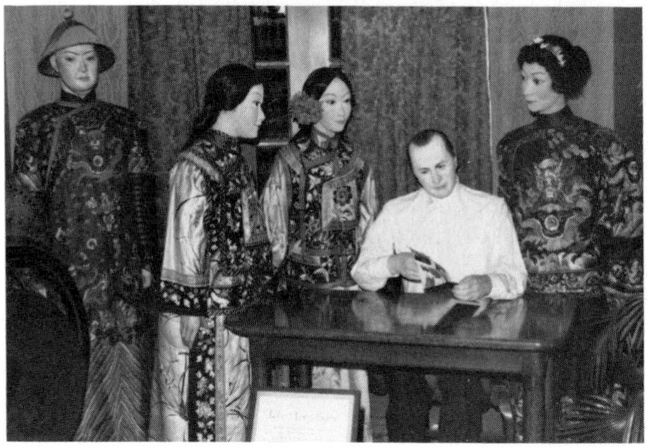

TOP, LEFT: Dr. Gardner's Museums of Witchcraft and Magic in San Francisco, California, and Gatlinburg, Tennessee, specialize in displays based on the mystic, and occasionally horrible, rites of the occult. Many of the objects on display in the two museums were collected by Dr. Gardner, the "King of British Witches," who died in 1964. He is represented in wax in the Museum of Witchcraft and Magic, San Francisco. CENTER: This Museum of Witchcraft and Magic presentation depicts an altar prepared for a Black Mass, a blasphemous parody of the Mass by worshipers of Satan. RIGHT: Two sixteenth-century psychics on view at Dr. Gardner's San Francisco museum: Dr. John Dee *(left)* and Edward Kelly.

CENTER, LEFT: Witches, old and young await visitors. Dr. Gardner's Museum of Witchcraft and Magic, San Francisco. RIGHT: Franciscan philosopher and scientist Roger Bacon. The thirteenth-century scholar was interested in all fields of knowledge, including the mystical. Dr. Gardner's Museum of Witchcraft and Magic, San Francisco.

BOTTOM, LEFT: Seven Ripley's Believe-It-or-Not museums (in San Francisco, California; Chicago, Illinois; St. Augustine, Florida; Gatlinburg, Tennessee; Estes Park, Colorado; Niagara Falls, Canada; and Blackpool, England) display curiosities collected by Robert Ripley of "Believe-It-or-Not" fame. In many of the exhibits wax figures are used to re-create famous Ripley cartons. Because Ripley began his career in San Francisco and that city was his headquarters for many years, the San Francisco Believe-It-or-Not Museum displays a re-creation of Ripley's studio where Ripley sits at a table surrounded by his Oriental servants. RIGHT: Little Jack Horner is a nursery rhyme character who appears in the Believe-It-or-Not museums with an explanation that he was a real person. Moreover, Jack did pull a "plum" out of a pie.

TOP, LEFT: Ripley's Locusta, "the witch" who served as a model for the Wicked Queen in the Grimm fairy tale "Snow White and the Seven Dwarfs." In real life, Locusta was an offical poisoner for Roman Emperor Nero. CENTER: Ripley's representation of Che Mah, the Chinese midget who was only 28 inches tall, includes Che Mah's pigtail which was 13 feet long. RIGHT: This Ripley exhibit is based on the true story of an old lady who sat on a nest of eggs for three weeks until they hatched.

BOTTOM, LEFT: Lie Ch'ung, who had double pupils in each eye, appears with the Dowager Empress of China who appointed him minister of state A.D. 995. CENTER: Clad in chains, world-famous magician Houdini stands at the entrance to the Houdini Magical Hall of Fame in Niagara Falls, Canada. The figure was modeled after one of the magician's favorite photographs. RIGHT: This Houdini Magical Hall of Fame exhibit demonstrates the magician's Chinese Water Torture Cell equipment. Houdini's escape from the water-filled metal and mahogany tank was considered his greatest escape feat. In the background at right is the poster used to advertise the Chinese Water Torture Cell. The Houdini museum contains nearly all the intriguing paraphernalia used by Houdini in his extraordinary career as a magician and escape artist.

MOVIES, TV, AND ART

11

Among the many subjects covered by wax museums, probably none arouse more interest than the exhibits devoted to the motion pictures and television shows that millions of Americans have enjoyed, featuring the actors and actresses who starred in them. The ability of the wax sculptor to reproduce Clark Gable's likeness as Rhett in *Gone With the Wind,* or the likeness of the young Judy Garland as Dorothy in *The Wizard of Oz*, is part of that appeal. One can see in these pages the skill of the exhibit designer in re-creating an authentic movie set or TV background for the wax figures, and the care with which they are costumed, sometimes with clothing actually worn in the performances.

Several wax museums devote all or almost all of their exhibits to motion pictures and stars, while others have a special section. Whether the number of exhibits is large or small, the medium of wax has proved to be uniquely suited to capturing the magic of show business.

The great works of art here are posed as they were painted, or the museum may re-create the scene in the artist's studio when the painting was in progress. They are characterized by painstaking attention to detail, which makes them seem to come alive.

MOVIES

Silent-screen actor Rudolph Valentino as the dashing gaucho Julio in *The Four Horsemen of the Apocalypse* at Houston's Classic Showcase. The 1921 movie made him a star.

TOP, LEFT: Valentino in *The Son of the Sheik,* 1946. Classic Showcase. RIGHT: Close-up of Charlie Chaplin in *The Gold Rush. Courtesy London Wax Museum of Boston*

CENTER, LEFT: Stan Laurel and Oliver Hardy in a vintage auto in the lobby of the Movieland Wax Museum at Niagara Falls, where the first of the great screen comedy teams greets visitors. RIGHT: Posed with a collection of still photographs from their films. *Courtesy Movie Wax Museum*

BOTTOM: W. C. Fields in his role as Professor Eustace Gargle in the 1936 film *Poppy. Courtesy Movieland Wax Museum (Buena Park)*

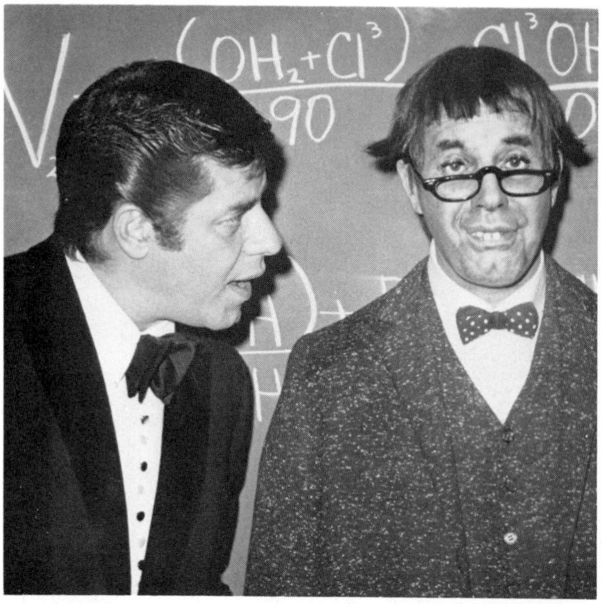

TOP, LEFT: The real Jerry Lewis examines Jerry Lewis the wax "Nutty Professor." Lewis donated the figure's wardrobe and teeth to the museum. *Courtesy Movieland Wax Museum* RIGHT: In its section devoted to movie stars, the Wax Museum at Fisherman's Wharf has assembled five of the screen's funniest men. *From left:* W.C. Fields, Stan Laurel, Bob Hope, Oliver Hardy, and Charlie Chaplin.

CENTER, LEFT: Cowboy stars who dominated the westerns of the 1920s and early 1930s seen against the backdrop of a typical movie saloon. *From left:* William S. Hart, Tom Mix, and Ken Maynard. *Courtesy Movieland Wax Museum (Buena Park)* CENTER, RIGHT: A saloon setting for western stars *(from left):* James Stewart, John Wayne, and Gary Cooper. Waxlife USA.

BOTTOM: Two generations of actors who starred in westerns *(from left):* Gary Cooper, Paul Newman, Robert Redford, and John Wayne. *Courtesy Wax Museum at Fisherman's Wharf*

TOP, LEFT: Gary Cooper and Grace Kelly in a scene from *High Noon.* Cooper received the 1952 best actor award for his role in that film. Movieland Wax Museum (Buena Park). CENTER: Gary Cooper at Houston's Classic Showcase. RIGHT: Vincent Price in House of Wax.

CENTER: Greta Garbo with a Duesenberg, Ginger Rogers on the running board of a Bentley, and Carole Lombard in a Duesenberg. Classic Showcase.

BOTTOM: Robert Redford *(left)* and Paul Newman in a scene from the 1969 production *Butch Cassidy and the Sundance Kid. Courtesy Movieland Wax Museum (Buena Park)*

TOP, LEFT: Illustrious leading lady Joan Crawford. Southwestern Historical Wax Museum. RIGHT: Peter Lorre *(left)* is about to stab Sidney Greenstreet. Niagara Falls Movieland Wax Museum's commemoration of the classic private-eye film *The Maltese Falcon.*

CENTER: Dorothy (Judy Garland) and her friends, the Tin Man (Jack Haley, Sr.), the Scarecrow (Ray Bolger), and the Cowardly Lion (Bert Lahr), from the 1939 film classic *The Wizard of Oz,* await visitors to *(from left)* the Movieland Wax Museum in Buena Park and the Movie Wax Museum at Estes Park. *Courtesy Movieland Wax Museum (Buena Park)* and *Movie Wax Museum*

BOTTOM: Kirk Douglas with his likeness. *Courtesy Movieland Wax Museum (Buena Park)*

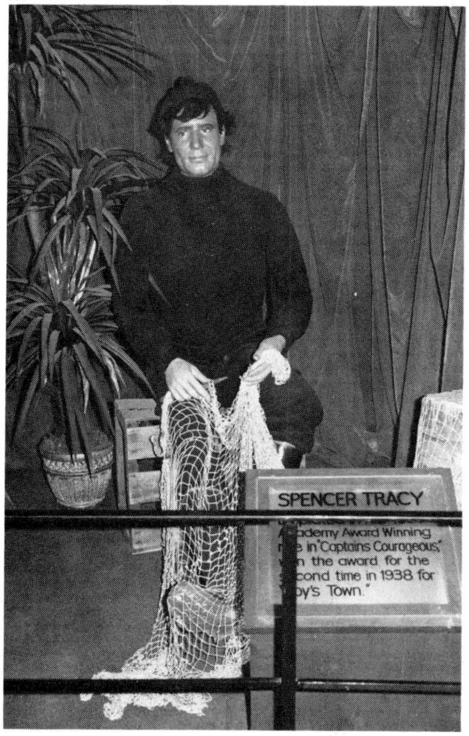

Through the medium of wax, stars of memorable movies of the 1930s re-create their roles at the Movieland Wax Museum (Buena Park). Seen here are Spencer Tracy in *Captains Courageous,* Robert Taylor and Hedy Lamarr in *Lady of the Tropics,* James Cagney and Pat O'Brien in *Angels with Dirty Faces,* Charles Laughton in *The Private Life of Henry VIII,* and William Powell and Myrna Loy in *The Thin Man.*

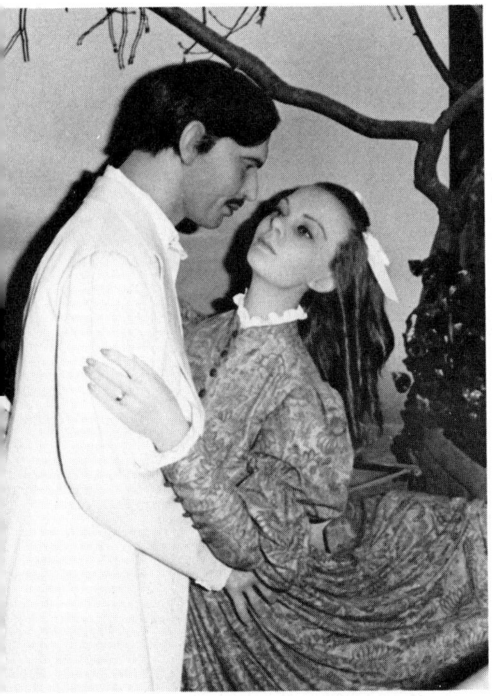

TOP: Clark Gable and Vivien Leigh in episodes from *Gone With the Wind,* one of the most famous motion pictures ever made: Underground Wax Museum *(left),* Waxlife USA *(center),* and the Josephine Tussaud Wax Museum of the *Queen Mary.*

BOTTOM, LEFT: Elizabeth Taylor and Richard Burton, stars of the multimillion-dollar epic *Cleopatra,* emote. *Courtesy Tokyo Tower Wax Museum* CENTER: Alan Ladd as Shane. Movieland Wax Museum (Buena Park). RIGHT: The Real Gloria Swanson *(right)* with her wax likeness during a visit. *Courtesy Movieland Wax Museum (Buena Park)*

TOP, LEFT AND CENTER: Close-ups of *The African Queen* stars Katherine Hepburn and Humphrey Bogart. Movieland Wax Museum (Buena Park). RIGHT: Yul Brynner as the King of Siam, the award-winning role he played in the movie *The King and I. Courtesy Movieland Wax Museum*

BOTTOM, LEFT: Rod Steiger's likeness is made up for the actor's role in the film *The Illustrated Man.* Movieworld Cars of the Stars. CENTER AND RIGHT: Film glamour queen Marilyn Monroe, who died in 1962, is a favorite wax museum subject. These likenesses of the star appear at *(left)* Madame Tussaud's in London (in her *Bus Stop* role) and Movie Wax Museum.

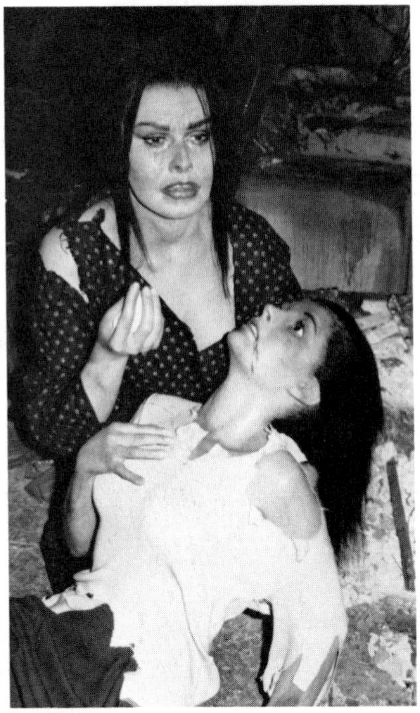

TOP, LEFT: Wax museum likeness of French "sex-kitten" Brigitte Bardot at Waxlife USA. CENTER: Clint Eastwood as the rough-and-ready lawman of *Dirty Harry.* Hollywood Wax Museum. RIGHT: Actor Steve McQueen. Wax Museum at Fisherman's Wharf.

CENTER, LEFT: *Singing in the Rain* star Gene Kelly appears to be doing just that. Movieland Wax Museum (Buena Park). CENTER AND RIGHT: Italian star Sophia Loren as she appears in Waxlife USA *(left)* and in a scene from *Two Women* at the Movieland Wax Museum (Buena Park).

BOTTOM: Cliff Robertson (clinging to rope) in a dramatic episode from *PT-109,* the 1963 movie in which Robertson played the role of Navy Lieutenant John F. Kennedy. Movieland Wax Museum (Buena Park).

Some leading ladies *(from top):* Barbra Streisand and a close-up of Gina Lollobrigida at the Movieland Wax Museum in Buena Park; Raquel Welch (in her *Fantastic Voyage* role) at the Hollywood Wax Museum; and Goldie Hawn at the Royal London Wax Museum in Phoenix. *Streisand photo courtesy Movieland Wax Museum (Buena Park)*

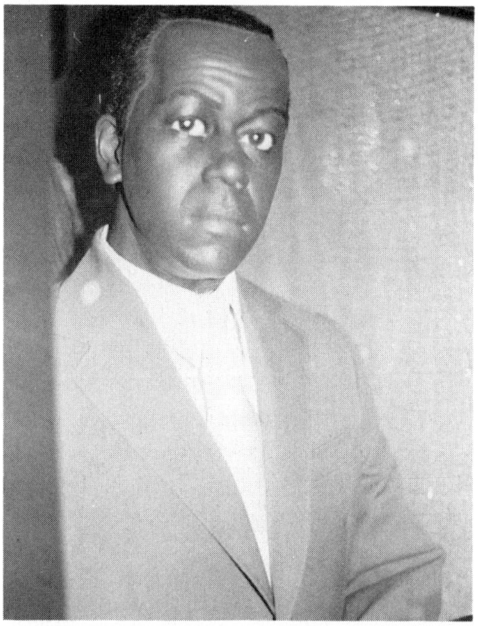

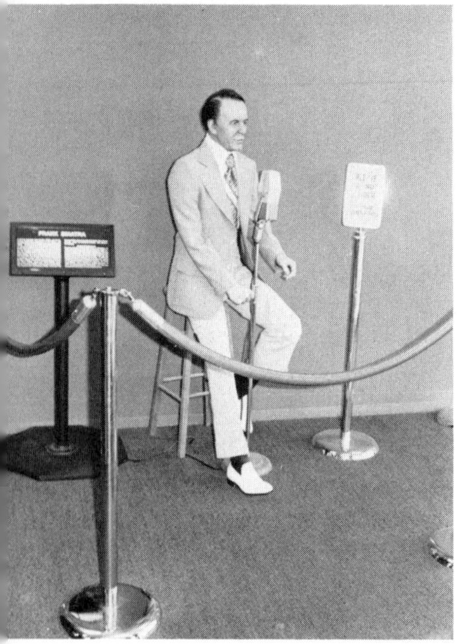

TOP: Well-known comedians the late Jack Benny, with his violin, Bob Hope, dressed in the uniform he wore while entertaining American troops overseas (Waxlife USA), and TV's Flip Wilson (Underground Wax Museum).

BOTTOM, LEFT: Frank Sinatra, whose career has also included motion pictures and television at Waxlife USA. CENTER AND RIGHT: Contralto Marian Anderson *(left)* and entertainer Lena Horne. *Louis Tussaud's English Wax Museum (Atlantic City).*

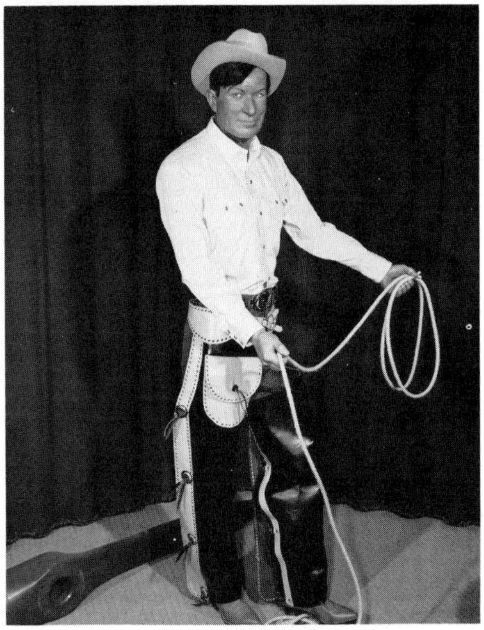

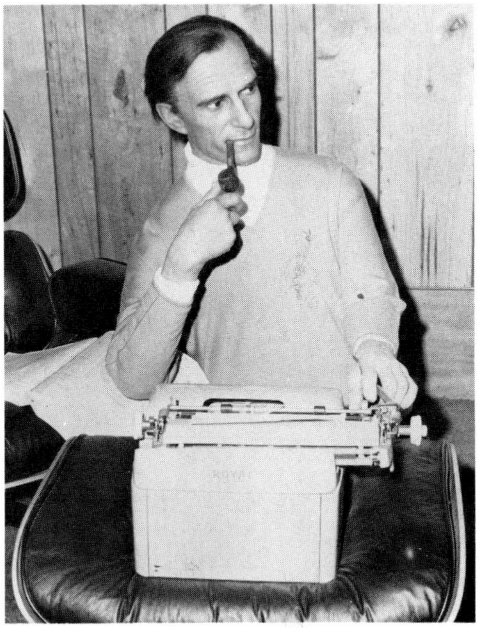

TOP: Four top-flight entertainers share the spotlight here. *From left:* talented singer and actress Barbra Streisand; Elvis Presley, still popular after twenty years in show business; Liza Minnelli, acclaimed for her motion-picture and television performances; and Sammy Davis, Jr., the versatile singer, dancer, and actor. *Courtesy Wax Museum at Fisherman's Wharf*

CENTER, LEFT: Janis Joplin. In 1970 this top-flight rock singer died a drug-related death. Toronto Wax Museum. CENTER: Will Rogers, the famous cowboy humorist, who began his show business career in vaudeville and went on to become a musical comedy and movie star. *Courtesy Southwestern Historical Wax Museum.* RIGHT: Chicago-born Hugh Hefner, the founder of *Playboy* magazine, the popular Playboy Clubs, and related enterprises. *Courtesy Royal London Wax Museum (Chicago)*

BOTTOM: Hefner "at home." *Courtesy Underground Wax Museum (Atlanta)*

MAE WEST

ACADEMY
"MIN & BILL"
MARIE DRESSLER
WALLACE BEERY

CO. M.G.M. 1934
"THE MERRY WIDOW"
JEANETTE MAC DONALD
MAURICE CHEVALIER
DIR. LUBITSCH
PROD. M.G.M.
SCENE No. 15 TAKE No. 3

"ANIMAL CRACKERS"
MARX BROTHERS
13

"DON'T FENCE ME IN"
ROY ROGERS
DALE EVANS
20 1

"HOUSE OF WAX"
VINCENT PRICE
22 8

A sampling of scenes from the $6-million project of Six Flags, Inc.—the Stars Hall of Fame wax museum in Orlando, Florida. More than 200 stars of motion picture, television, and song are presented in its history of entertainment. A sister museum to the Movieland Wax Museum in Buena Vista, California, the Stars Hall of Fame is on a seven-acre site near the Walt Disney World in Florida.

TELEVISION

TOP, LEFT: Longtime television impresario Ed Sullivan in a typical pose. During his twenty-three years as host of TV's most popular variety show, Sullivan presented a legion of entertainers to TV audiences. Louis Tussaud's English Wax Museum (Atlantic City). RIGHT: The Beatles, one of the many musical groups introduced to American TV audiences by Ed Sullivan. The Beatles appear as they did at the time of their first U.S. performances in 1964. *From left:* Paul McCartney, George Harrison, Ringo Starr, and John Lennon. Louis Tussaud's English Wax Museum (Atlantic City).

CENTER, LEFT: Carroll O'Connor, Archie Bunker of the popular TV series "All in the Family," in the lobby at Louis Tussaud's English Wax Museum at Niagara Falls. RIGHT: A reproduction of a set used in the long-running television series "Bonanza" and three of "Bonanza's" stars. *From left:* Michael Landon, Lorne Greene, Dan Blocker. *Courtesy Movieland Wax Museum (Buena Park)*

BOTTOM: A set for the TV series "Star Trek." Movieland Wax Museum (Buena Park).

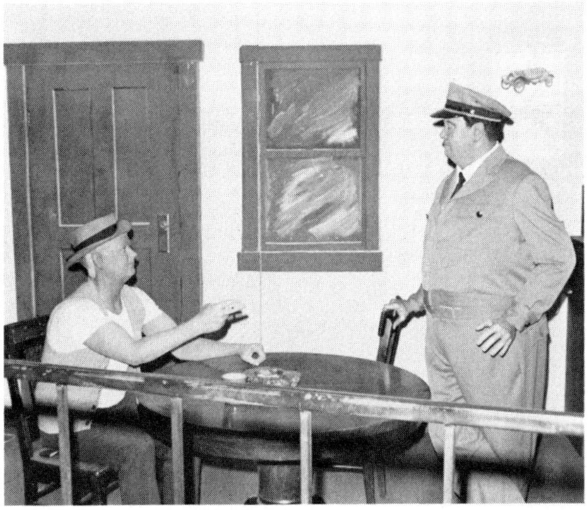

TOP, LEFT: At Houston's Classic Showcase a "Honeymooners" set has been constructed for Art Carney *(left)* and Jackie Gleason, the stars of that hilarious series. CENTER AND RIGHT: TV talk show hosts *(left)* David Frost and Merv Griffin. Madame Tussaud's in London and Louis Tussaud's English Wax Museum (Atlantic City).

CENTER: Three funny lady TV stars *(from left):* Lucille Ball at Movieland Wax Museum in Buena Park and Phyllis Diller and Carol Burnett at Louis Tussaud's English Wax Museum in Atlantic City.

BOTTOM, LEFT: Real comedians Dan Rowan *(left)* and Dick Martin pose with their lifelike effigies. *Courtesy Movieland Wax Museum (Buena Park)*
RIGHT: TV personality Cher as she appears at the Hollywood Wax Museum in Buena Park.

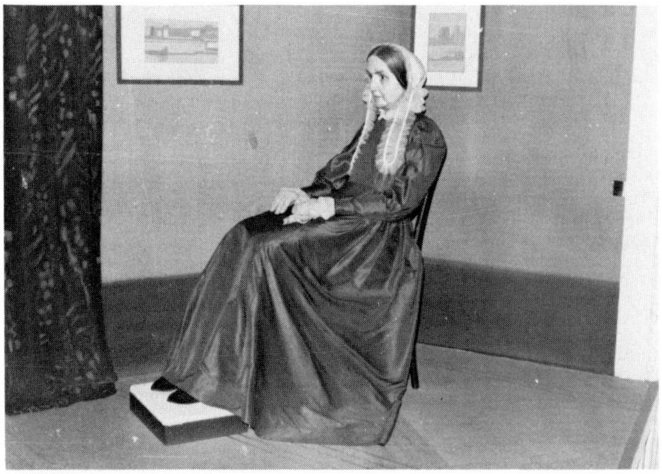

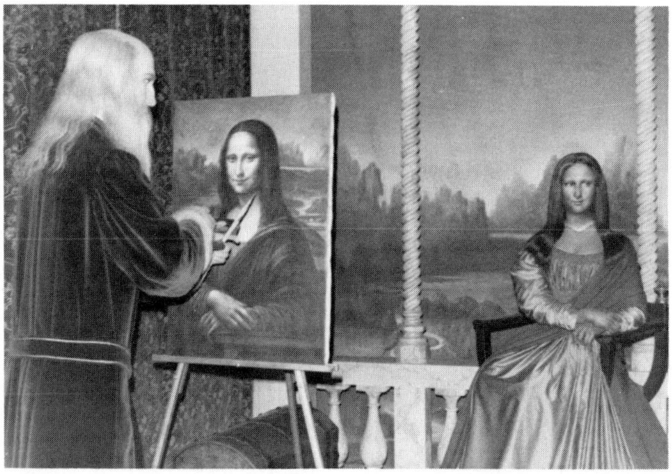

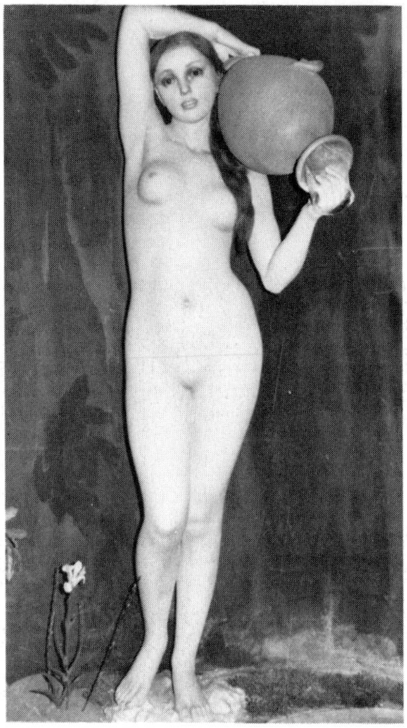

ART

TOP, LEFT: Whistler's mother at the Palace of Living Art at the Movieland Wax Museum in Buena Park where reproductions of noted sculptures and more than two dozen famous paintings are brought to life through the medium of wax, as seen in the following illustrations. RIGHT: Mona Lisa posing for Leonardo da Vinci.

CENTER, LEFT: Copies of well-known paintings are paired with three-dimensional wax reproductions. Compare Thomas Gainsborough's "The Blue Boy" with the museum's. CENTER: Jean-Auguste-Dominique Ingres's painting "La Source" in wax. Ingres worked thirty-two years to capture what he considered the ultimate in feminine beauty. RIGHT: Brightness, Joy, and Bloom, the subjects of Hyacinthe Rigaud's "The Three Graces," as they appear in wax.

BOTTOM: This wax figure is based on Rigaud's portrait of French King Louis XIV. Parisian artisans created the figure, costume, and background. *Courtesy Palace of Living Art*

TOP, LEFT: The museum has reproduced the room depicted in Vincent van Gogh's "The Artist's Room at Arles" and in it placed a figure based on van Gogh's self-portrait. CENTER: This lovely figure of a young girl was modeled in wax after Sir Thomas Lawrence's portrait "Pinkie," which he completed in 1795. RIGHT *(left)*: The Palace of Living Art's reproduction of the famous Venus de Milo. *Right:* A wax likeness of Venus as she might have appeared while posing for the sculptor of the original statute. *Courtesy Palace of Living Art*

CENTER, LEFT: Don Quixote and Sancho Panza make their way through the museum. RIGHT: Grant Wood's farm couple from "American Gothic" translated into three-dimensional wax figures. The painting is a copy.

BOTTOM: The Palace of Living Art's wax reproduction of Heinrich Hofmann's "Christ in the Garden of Gethsemane."

COUNTRY WESTERN MUSIC STARS

12

Country western music has millions of followers in the United States and abroad. From its humble beginning as the self-made country music of the poor, poverty-stricken, and lonely people of the hill country and the South, it moved west where it joined forces with western music, ending in the northeast with newly found acceptance. More hit songs and tunes come out of Nashville—Home of Country Music—than anywhere else.

The success formula for this music form is the combinations of vocals, songwriting, and instrumentation, and depends on the mood it strikes with the audience. It can be nostalgic, gospel, kind or cruel, funny, full of protest, a story with or without a moral, a love story, or a sad commentary on one's personal life, all part of country western's charm and appeal. It is music of the people, by the people, for the people.

These scenes, mainly from the Country Music Wax Museum in Nashville, are highlighted with unusual lighting and are in glass enclosures. Photographs from other museums will be indicated in the captions.

EARLY COUNTRY WESTERN MUSIC

RIGHT: Stephen Foster, thought of by many American historians as the "Father of Country Music," composing a song at the National Historical Wax Museum, Washington, D.C. FAR RIGHT: Stephen Foster in a garden along the Swannee River (Florida) at the Underground Wax Museum in Atlanta. Foster developed songs from music he had heard in a black church in Pennsylvania. Some of his songs are "Open Thy Lattice, Love," and "O! Susanna." Later, others unfolded from the "colored church music": "Massa's in de Cold Ground," "My Old Kentucky Home," and "Old Black Joe." His wife, Jane, eventually left him, in spite of a beautiful song he wrote about her expressing his love ("Jeanie with the Light Brown Hair"). At the age of thirty-eight, in the Bowery of New York City, he succumbed to her loss.

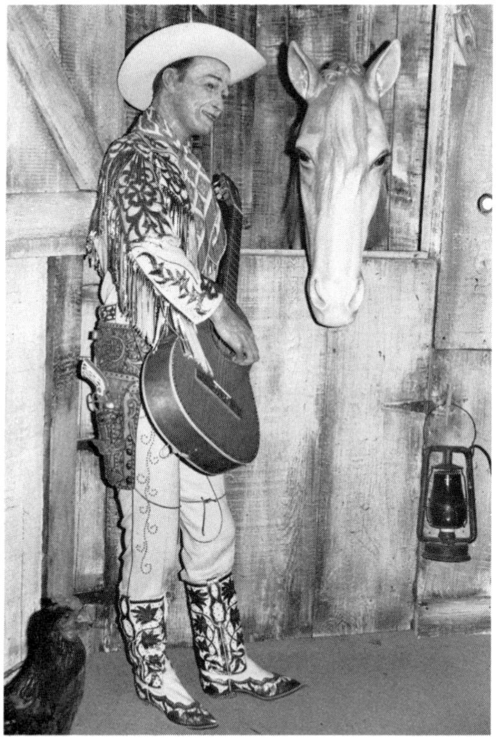

TOP, LEFT: Roy Rogers serenading his horse, Trigger. Roy deposed Gene Autry in 1940 as the movies' "King of the Singing Cowboys." There were many singing cowboys during the 1930s and 1940s but these two and Tex Ritter made millions out of it. Another was Spade Cooley who became "King of Western Swing" and is credited with moving western music far enough toward country for a merger. Movieland Wax Museum.

THE GRAND OLE OPRY

CENTER, TOP: The Grand Ole Opry is the hometown temple of the country music cult and it had its beginning in Nashville on November 28, 1925, when the National Life Insurance Company launched the first radio station WSM Barn Dance. On that first program was an eighty-year-old fiddler named Uncle Jimmy Thompson and an announcer called Judge (George D.) Hay. They are seen here with "Dixie Dewdrop"—Uncle Dave Macon, the "Grandaddy of the Opry," who joined them in 1926 and played a banjo "like no one else in the world" for twenty-five years in the Opry until his death in 1952. BOTTOM: The Grand Ole Opry by 1940 overtook the Chicago National Barn Dance throughout the country as the number one country music show. That year the Opry had Clell Summey introduce the electric steel guitar, and Minnie Pearl, "Queen of Country Comedy," joined the show. She is seen here with comedian Rod Brasfield (who joined the Opry in 1944).

RIGHT, TOP: In 1948, the already famous Hank Williams joined the regulars on the Opry show. Two years later he was fired for drunkenness and on January 1, 1953 (at the age of twenty-nine), died before he could be rehired. He was honored by being placed in the Country Music Hall of Fame in its first year, 1961. Williams had achieved his initial fame while singing with the "Junior Grande Ole Opry" and the Louisiana Hayride in Shreveport and Little Rock. He was an instant hit at the Opry, and in his short life was more popular than any other country music star. BOTTOM: Midwestern Hayride, Cincinnati, started in 1938 as Boone county Jamboree and featured such acts as Merle Travis. This is where he got his big boost to fame as a country music star. His outstanding early effort was "Folk Songs from the Hills" in 1947.

TOP, LEFT: Sonny James, another superstar, who came from the Tennessee Bar Dance at Knoxville. CENTER: "The Famous Carter Family" was one of the most important acts in country music. A.P., Mother Maybelle *(seated)* and Sara are seen here. A.P. in his early years collected an extensive amount of Appalachian ballad material, which he turned into recordings. Maybelle was married to A.P.'s brother Ezra and Sara was married to A.P. They started recording in 1927 and did their last record together in 1941. RIGHT: June Carter, daughter of Ezra and Maybelle, married Johnny Cash in 1968. Both are outstanding country music stars. Johnny Cash, a superstar, has many million-selling record hits. From a 1955 start with the Opry, he went on to his own television show in the 1960s where he was a smash hit for years. He and June won Grammies for Best Group Performance in 1967 and 1970.

BOTTOM, LEFT: Johnny Wright *(seated)* and Jack Anglin *(right)* had one of the top entertainment acts going, called Johnny and Jack, when Jack was killed in an automobile accident on the way to Opry Star Patsy Cline's funeral. Patsy, Cowboy Copas, and Hawkshaw Hawkins, Opry greats, were killed in 1962 in a plane crash. Johnny then teamed up with his wife, Kitty Wells, to produce and star in their very successful television and road show. RIGHT: The Grand Ole Opry stage with a collection of some of its all-time greats *(left):* Whitey Ford (Duke of Paduca), Bill Carlisle, Pop Stoneman, Cowboy Copas, hidden from view by Roy Acuff, and Patsy Cline.

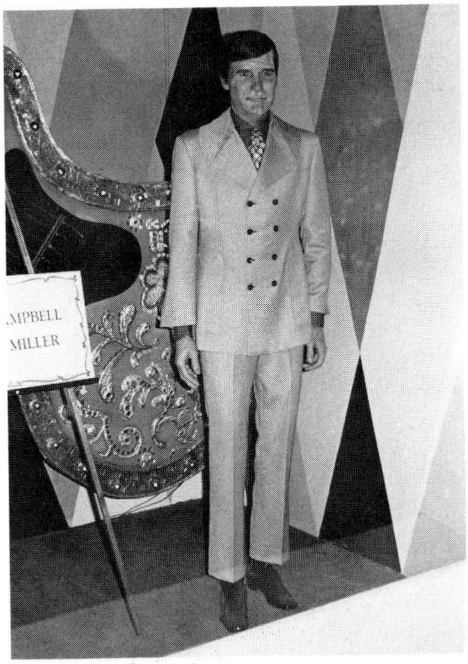

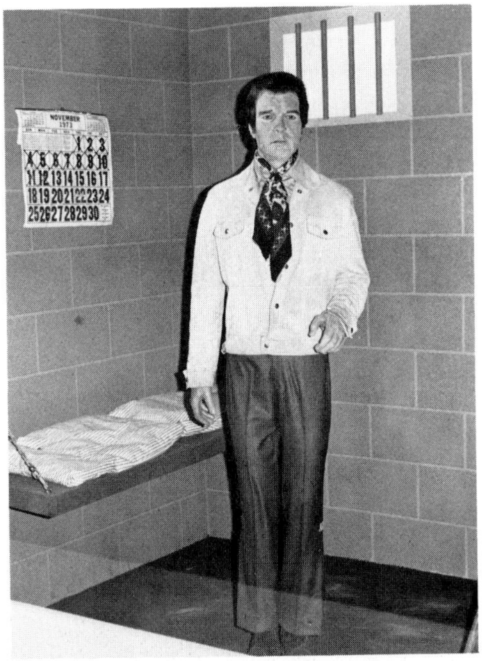

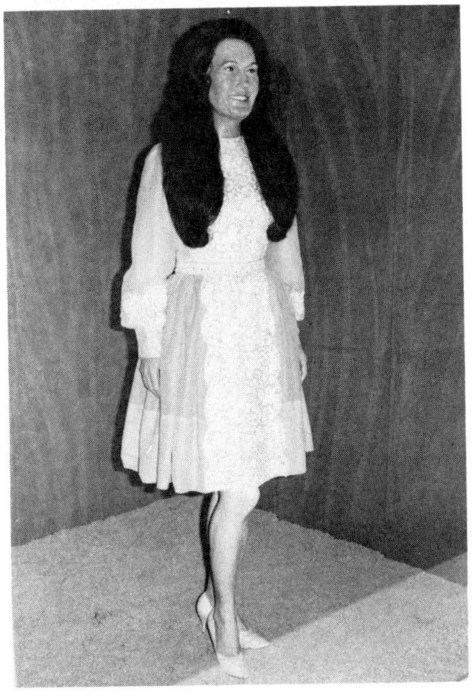

LATER COUNTRY MUSIC SUPERSTARS

TOP, LEFT: Roger Miller, a great songwriter and singer. Three of his gold record (million sales list) songs were *"Dang Me," "Chug-A-Lug,"* and, of course, *"King of the Road."* In 1964 and 1965 he won seven Grammy awards with these three songs. RIGHT: Merle Haggard, a superstar, entered the country music scene late (1965) but soon had a number of hits and today is one of the top stars in country music.

BOTTOM, LEFT: Loretta Lynn, country music superstar, was named the Top Female Vocalist in 1971 and 1973 by the Academy of Country Music and was the Country Music Hall of Fame's winner of the Female Vocalist of the Year award in 1967, 1972, and 1973. CENTER: Glen Campbell, a superstar in both country music and pop, as a musician knocked around Nashville for years (since grade school) until he finally hit it big in 1967 with a million sale song, "Gentle on My Mind." Tops among his best sellers are "By the Time I Get to Phoenix" and "Galveston." He then had his own musical television show. In 1967 he won three Grammy awards with the song "Gentle on My Mind." RIGHT: Charlie Pride, the first black to become a country music superstar (in the late 1960s) was once a professional baseball player, like Roy Acuff and Jim Reeves. His first big hit was "Does My Ring Hurt Your Finger?" followed by many more smash hits. In 1972 he won a Grammy as Best Male Vocalist with the album *Charlie Pride Sings Heart Songs.*

RELIGIONS 13

One dictionary definition for religion is "a reverence for the gods, holiness, in a system of religious belief—a belief in a divine or superhuman power or powers to be obeyed and worshiped as the creator(s) and ruler(s) of the universe with an expression of such a belief in conduct and ritual." Blending this definition with the fact that man, since the beginning of civilization, has sought a meaning to his life suggests that he is looking for a Supreme Being. The roads he has traveled have been diverse—Hinduism, Taoism, Buddhism, Islam, Judaism, and Christianity. These great religions are represented in wax museums throughout the world, some devoting their entire space to religion. The Wax Museum at Fisherman's Wharf has a Hall of Religions, with exhibits on all these religions; Christus Gardens is not actually a wax museum (although its figures are of wax made by Keith Gems) but a temple of religious meditation; and the recently opened Musée de Cire Lourdes in Lourdes, France, offers a portrayal of the lives of Christ and Bernadette.

HINDUISM

Hindu worshipers in this scene practice their ancient rite of cleansing in the Ganges River, whose waters they believe purify and heal. Hindus believe their religion is the source of all major religions and that God dwells within them and that He may be reached by the fourfold path of knowledge, love, work, and meditation. *Courtesy Wax Museum at Fisherman's Wharf*

TAOISM

TOP, LEFT: When the ancient philospher Lao Tzu left China in the sixth century B.C. astride a water buffalo, his thoughts remained behind in the Tao Te Ching, which soon became the bible for a vast new philosophy/religion known as Taoism. Essentially, Taoism declares that true reality is the reality that can be contacted only through contemplation. Over the years, Taoism became the vehicle for many of the primitive magical cults of rural China. But now it shares with Confucianism the fate of being replaced in mainland China by the sterile idol of Marxism which may in the realm of things disappear in a relatively short period of civilization. Then, for the vast majority of the 500 million Chinese who are estimated to still believe in Confucianism and Taoism, there will be a return to the teachings of K'ung Fu-Tzu and Lao Tzu. *Courtesy Wax Museum at Fisherman's Wharf*

BUDDHISM

TOP, RIGHT: This Buddha is in the Royal London Wax Museum in Phoenix. Buddha, who lived in the fifth century B.C. as Prince Siddhartha Gautama, left his life of luxury and set out to seek a deeper meaning of life. While he sat meditating under a Bodhi tree, the devil Mara came to him and offered him all of the wealth in the world if he would discontinue his quest. Gautama refused to give up his search and forty-nine days later the Truth was revealed to him. He became known as the Enlightened One—the Buddha. This gentle and peaceable religion was essentially a protestant revolt against orthodox Hinduism, preaching a middle ground between austerity and self-indulgence.

ISLAM

RIGHT, TOP: In A.D. 630 the Prophet Mohammed returned to the city of Mecca, on the Arabian coast of the Red Sea, from his eight-year exile in Medina, 200 miles to the north. Joined by an army of many thousands of enthusiastic new converts, Mohammed set about destroying the idols in the city and thereby firmly established the newest of the great religions. In deference to the Islamic ban on showing representations of the great Prophet, only his back is shown in this wax scene. Mohammed declared that there were Five Pillars of Islam, duties to be carried out by the True Believer: 1. Proclamation of the unity of God: "There is no God but Allah; Mohammed is the Messenger of Allah"; 2. Prayer five times daily, always facing the Holy City of Mecca; 3. Almsgiving; 4. The fast of the Holy Month of Ramadan; 5. The pilgrimage to Mecca. *Courtesy Wax Museum at Fisherman's Wharf*

JUDAISM AND CHRISTIANITY

Moses was the great religious and national leader of the Jewish people. He received the Ten Commandments on Mount Sinai from the One God, Jahveh. This set of ethical and religious precepts has become the most important code in the world, paramount as it is to both Judaism and Christianity. The Ten Commandments are to be found in the Book of Exodus, and for nearly 14 million Jews (half of whom live in the United States) this is the core of Torah—their law. Christianity is the religion of one-third of the population on earth. More than one billion human beings are identified in one way or another with the Christian movement. Christianity begins with Jesus Christ. The effects of His life, the response to His teachings and the experience and nature of His death and resurrection were the beginnings of the Christian community, and the Ten Commandements have been the foundation for its religious beliefs ever since. RIGHT, CENTER: Adam and Eve. National Historical Was Museum. BOTTOM: Abraham about to sacrifice his son Isaac. National Historical Wax Museum.

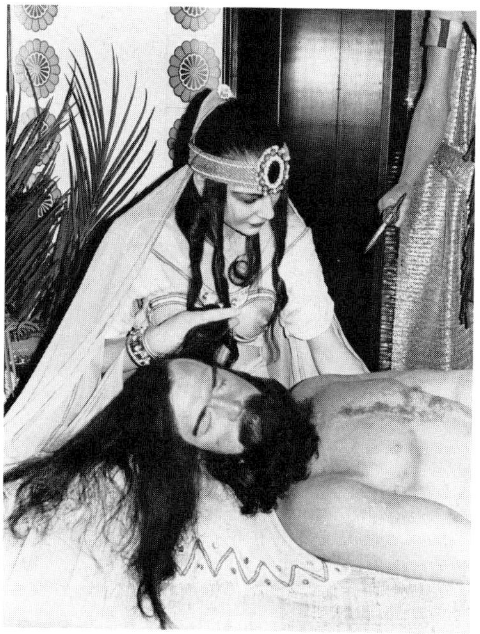

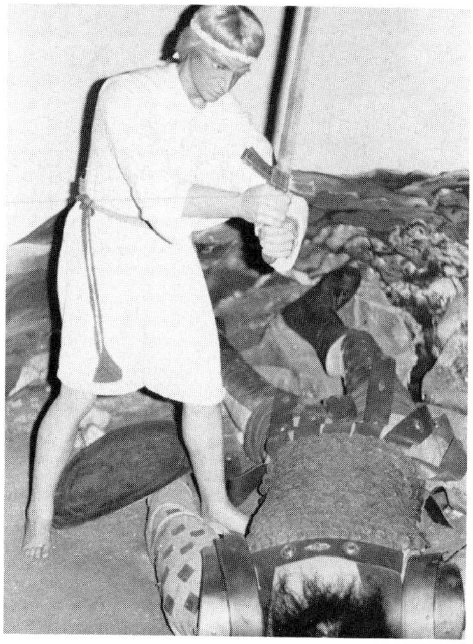

TOP, LEFT: Moses, the revered religious and national leader of the Jewish people, is shown as he receives the Ten Commandments on Mount Sinai. Underground Wax Museum. RIGHT: Delilah and Samson. Louis Tussaud's English Wax Museum (Atlantic City).

CENTER, LEFT: David slays Goliath. National Historical Wax Museum. RIGHT: Manger scene with the Three Wise Men presenting gifts to the Christ Child. Biblical Wax Museum, Niagara Falls, Canada.

BOTTOM: The Sermon on the Mount. Underground Wax Museum.

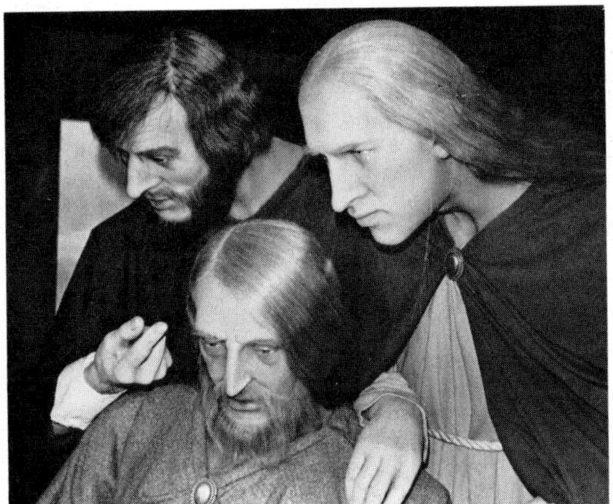

Thirteen wax museums have a Last Supper scene, making it the most popular of all. Each is done with great fidelity to the original famous painting by Leonardo da Vinci, created by the master in 1495 for the Church of Santa Maria delle Grazie in Milan, Italy. Jesus is with His original twelve apostles. The photographs on this page were taken at Christus Gardens, London Wax Museum of Boston, Pioneer Square Wax Museum, and the Josephine Tussaud Wax Museum at Hot Springs. TOP: Leonardo da Vinci's "Last Supper" re-created in a forty-foot diorama with wax figures representing Christ and the Twelve Apostles *(left to right):* Bartholomew, James the Younger, Andrew, Peter *(behind Judas),* John, Jesus, Thomas, James the Elder, Philip, Matthew, Thaddaeus, and Simon. *Courtesy Christus Gardens.* SECOND ROW: Bartholomew; James the Younger and Andrew; Judas, Peter, John, and Jesus. THIRD ROW: Thomas, James the Elder, Philip; Matthew; Thaddaeus; and Simon.

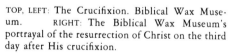

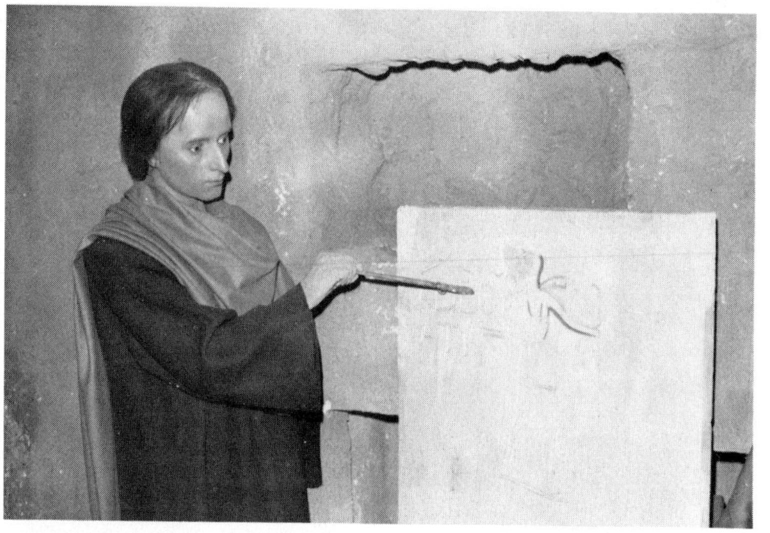

TOP, LEFT: The Crucifixion. Biblical Wax Museum. RIGHT: The Biblical Wax Museum's portrayal of the resurrection of Christ on the third day after His crucifixion.

CENTER: A life-size wax figure in a scene based on the history of the early Christian Church. The wax artist is in the Catacombs of Rome working on a tomb inscription. The museum's reconstruction of the Catacombs includes accurate reproductions of tombstomes, frescoes, paintings, and lamps. Musée Historique Canadien Ltée.

BOTTOM: A baptism by immersion in the Catacombs.

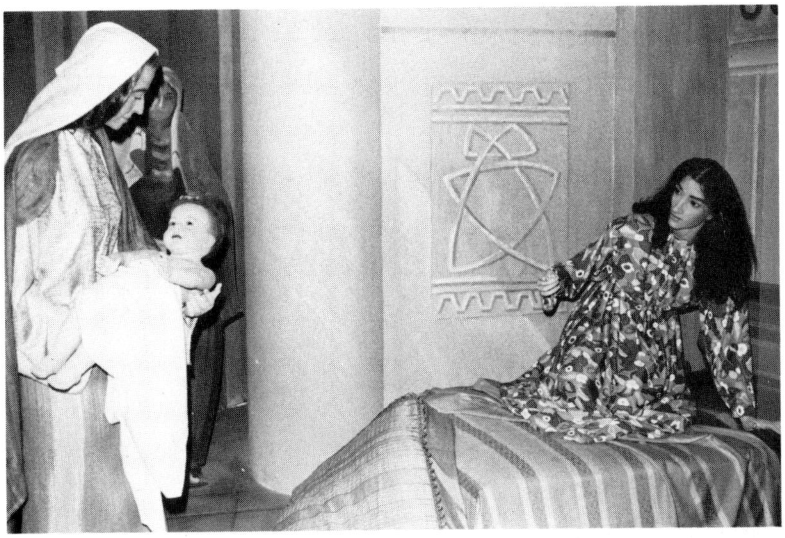

TOP, LEFT: In its Basilica Wax Museum, or Historial, the Shrine of Sainte Anne de Beaupré has used wax figures to tell the story of Saint Anne, the mother of Mary, and the history of her shrine at Beaupré. Seen here are Saint Anne *(left)* and the infant Mary. RIGHT: The first miraculous cure in the history of Sainte Anne de Beaupré: a farmer *(right)* who, in 1658, after placing three small stones in the first chapel's foundation was no longer crippled.

BOTTOM, LEFT: John Wesley, father of Methodism. Potter's Wax Museum. CENTER: Arthur Michael Ramsey, Archbishop of Canterbury. Louis Tussaud's Wax Museum at Niagara Falls, Canada. RIGHT: *(Left)* Martin Luther, the Augustinian monk who founded the Lutheran Church, and Roger Williams *(right),* who founded Providence, R.I., first English colony to grant religious freedom. Potter's Wax Museum.

DIRECTORY OF WAX MUSEUMS

(Operating schedules are subject to change.) Prepared with the help of G. C. Krueger, Jr., Secretary, International Association of Wax Museums, 1419 North Wells Street, Chicago, Illinois 60610. Most of the museums are members of the Association.

UNITED STATES

Arizona

FLAGSTAFF

Fort McClurg Wax Museum, Route 1, Box 932. Fort Flagstaff, Ariz. 86001 (tel.: 602-685-1670). (Located on Highway 89 North, in Flagstaff.) Hours: summer—7:30 A.M.-9:30 P.M.; winter—8 A.M.-6 P.M.

PHOENIX

Royal London Wax Museum, 5555 E. Van Buren, Phoenix, Ariz. 85005 (tel.: 602-273-1368). (Located near Sky Harbor International Airport.) Hours: open daily 9:30 A.M.-9:30 P.M.

Arkansas

HOT SPRINGS

Josephine Tussaud Wax Museum, 250 Central Avenue, Hot Springs, Ark. 71901 (tel.: 501-623-5836). (Located at Hot Springs National Park in downtown Hot Springs.) Hours: Feb. 1 through Labor Day—9 A.M.-10 P.M.; remainder of year—9 A.M.-6 P.M.

California

✓ ANAHEIM

Disneyland, Anaheim, Cal. 92802 (tel.: 714-533-4456). (Located 26 miles south of Los Angeles on Harbor Blvd. off the Santa Ana Freeway.) Hours: daily—8 A.M.-midnight.

BUENA PARK

Movieworld Cars of the Stars, 6920 Orangethorpe, Buena Park, Cal. 90620 (tel.: 714-523-1520). Hours: daily—10 A.M.-10 P.M.

Movieland Wax Museum and Palace of Living Art, 7711 Beach Boulevard, Buena Park, Cal. 90620 (tel.: 714-522-1154). Hours: summer—9 A.M.-10 P.M., Friday and Saturday-11 P.M.; winter—10 A.M.-9 P.M., Friday and Saturday to 11 P.M.

HOLLYWOOD

Hollywood Wax Museum, 6767 Hollywood Boulevard, Hollywood, Cal. 90028 (tel.: 213-462-5991). Hours: open daily 10 A.M. to midnight, Friday and Saturday to 2 A.M.

LONG BEACH

Josephine Tussaud Wax Museum of the Queen Mary, No. 39 *Queen Mary* Pier J, Long Beach, Cal. 90802 (tel.: 213-437-1963). Hours: open daily 10 A.M.-11 P.M.

SAN FRANCISCO

Chinatown Wax Museum, 601 Grant Avenue, San Francisco, Cal. 94108 (tel.: 415-392-1011). Located in San Francisco's Chinatown.) Hours: open daily 10 A.M.-11 P.M.

Dr. Gardner's Museum of Witchcraft & Magic, 235 Jefferson Street, Fisherman's Wharf, San Francisco, Cal. 94133 (tel.: 415-673-9765). Hours: winter—Monday through Thursday 11 A.M.-10 P.M. Friday 11 A.M. to midnight. Saturday 10 A.M. to midnight. Sunday 10 A.M.-10 P.M. Summer—9 A.M.-11 P.M. weekdays, 9 A.M. to midnight Sunday.

Ripley's Believe It or Not! Museum, 175 Jefferson Street, Fisherman's Wharf, San Francisco, Cal. 94133 (tel.: 415-771-6188). Hours: winter—10 A.M.-10 P.M. Sunday through Thursday. Saturday—10 A.M. to midnight. Summer—9 A.M.-11 P.M. weekdays, 9 A.M. to midnight weekends.

Wax Museum at Fisherman's Wharf, 145 Jefferson Street, San Francisco, Cal. 94108 (tel.: 415-885-4834). Hours: summer (May 15 to Sept. 15—9 A.M.-11 P.M., Friday and Saturday to midnight; winter (Sept. 15-May 15)—10 A.M.-10 P.M., Friday and Saturday to 11 P.M.

Wharf Wax Museum, 275 Jefferson Street, San Francisco, Cal. 94108 (tel.: 415-776-6437). Hours: summer—9 A.M.-11 P.M., Friday and Saturday to midnight; winter—9:30 A.M.-10 P.M.

Colorado

COLORADO SPRINGS

Hall of Presidents Wax Museum, 1050 South 21st Street, Colorado Springs, Colo. 80904 (tel.: 303-635-3553). Hours: June 1 to Sept. 15—8 A.M.-10 P.M.; remainder of year—9 A.M.-6 P.M.

DENVER

The Wax Museum, 919 Bannock Street, Denver, Colo. 80204 (tel.: 303-255-7941). (Located one mile south of downtown area.) Hours: Memorial Day through Labor Day—9 A.M.-9 P.M.; remainder of year—10 A.M.-5 P.M.

ESTES PARK

Movie Wax Museum, 380 West Riverside Drive, Estes Park, Colo. 80517 (tel.: 303-586-3607). Hours: open May 15 through Nov. 1—Sunday through Thursday 10 A.M.-9 P.M., Friday and Saturday 10 A.M.-11 P.M.

Ripley's Believe It or Not! Museum, 145 Elkhorn Avenue, Estes Park, Colo. 80517 (tel.: 303-586-2726). Hours: open daily 10 A.M.-10 P.M. May-Nov. Closed rest of year.

MANITOU SPRINGS

Buffalo Bill Wax Museum, 400 West Manitou Avenue, Manitou Springs, Colo. 80829 (tel.: 303-685-5900). Hours: open daily 8 A.M.-10 P.M.

District of Columbia

✓ **National Historical Wax Museum,** 333 E Street, S.W., Washington, D.C. 20001 (tel.: 202-554-2600). Hours: open daily 9 A.M.-10 P.M., to 8 P.M. after Labor Day.

✓ **First Ladies Hall,** Smithsonian Institution, Washington, D.C. 20005 (tel.: 202-628-4422). Hours: summer—10 A.M.-9 P.M.; winter—10 A.M.-5:30 P.M.

Florida

CLERMONT

House of Presidents, 123 N. Highway 27, Clermont, Fla. 32711 (tel.: 904-394-2836). (Located adjacent to Citrus Tower.) Hours: open daily 8 A.M.-6 P.M. (Closed for two weeks after Labor Day.)

MIAMI

Miami Wax Museum, 13899 Biscayne Boulevard, N. Miami Beach, Fla. 33161 (tel.: 305-945-3641). Hours: Monday through Saturday—9:30 A.M.-9:30 P.M., Sunday—10 A.M.-9:30 P.M.

ORLANDO

Stars Hall of Fame, 6825 Starway Drive, Orlando, Fla. 32809 (tel.: 305-351-1120). (Located off Route 4.) Hours: summer (June 1 to Sept. 1)—Sunday through Thursday—9 A.M.-11 P.M., Friday and Saturday—9 A.M. to midnight; winter (Sept. 1 to June 1)—10 A.M.-10 P.M. every day.

✓ **Walt Disney World,** Lake Buena Vista, Orlando, Fla. 32809 (tel.: 305-824-4321). (Located 15 miles southwest of Orlando on U.S. 192.) Hours: daily 8 A.M. to midnight; winter—10 A.M.-6 P.M.

ST. AUGUSTINE

Potter's Wax Museum, Plaza Hotel, 1 King Street, St. Augustine, Fla. 32084 (tel.: 904-VA9-9056). (Located on the Plaza.) Hours: Monday through Saturday—9 A.M.-9 P.M., Sunday—1 P.M.-9 P.M.

Ripley's Believe It or Not! Museum, 19 San Marco Avenue, St. Augustine, Fla. 32084 (tel.: 904-824-1742). (Located near City Gate in old Castle Warden.) Hours: open daily 8 A.M.-10 P.M.

✓ ST. PETERSBURG

London Wax Museum, 5505 Gulf Boulevard, St. Petersburg Beach, Fla. 33706 (tel.: 813-360-6985). Hours: open daily 9 A.M.-9 P.M.

Georgia

✓ ATLANTA

Underground Wax Museum, 90 Alabama Street, Atlanta, Ga. 30303 (tel.: 404-524-6225). (Located in "Underground Atlanta.") Hours: Monday through Saturday—11 A.M.-11 P.M., Sunday—11 A.M.-5 P.M.

Illinois

CHICAGO

Ripley's Believe It or Not! Museum, 1500 North Wells Street, Chicago, Ill. 61610 (tel.: 312-337-6077). (Located in Old Town.) Hours: daily from noon to midnight.

Royal London Wax Museum, 1419 N. Wells Street, Chicago, Ill. 60610 (tel.: 312-337-7787). Hours: summer—12 noon-11 P.M., Fridays and Saturdays to 1 A.M. After Labor Day—12 noon-9 P.M.

Kentucky

CAVE CITY

Mammoth Cave Wax Museum, Box 306, Cave City, Ky. 42127 (tel.: 502-773-6783). (Located on Ky 70 at I-65.) Hours: May through Sept.—8:30 A.M.-9 P.M.; remainder of year—9 A.M.-5 P.M.

Louisiana

NEW ORLEANS

Musée Conti, 917 Conti Street, New Orleans, La. 70112 (tel.: 504-525-2605). Hours: Apr. to Sept. 3—9:30 A.M.-9 P.M.; remainder of year—10 A.M.-6 P.M., Saturdays, Sundays, and holidays to 9:15 P.M.

Maryland

ANNAPOLIS

Annapolis Naval Historical Wax Museum, 110 Dock Street, Annapolis, Md. 21401 (tel.: 301-268-7727). (Located on the city dock.) Hours: Nov. through Apr.—10 A.M.-6 P.M.; May through Oct.—9 A.M.-9 P.M.

Massachusetts

BOSTON

✓ **London Wax Museum of Boston,** 179 Tremont Street, Boston, Mass. 02111 (tel.: 617-542-6882). (Located opposite the Boston Common.) Hours: Monday through Saturday—10 A.M.-9:30 P.M., Sunday—1 P.M.-9:30 P.M.

✓ PLYMOUTH

Plymouth National Wax Museum, 16 Carver Street, Plymouth, Mass. 02360 (tel.: 617-746-6468). Hours: (open Mar. 1 to Dec. 1) summer—9 A.M.-9:30 P.M.; spring and fall—9 A.M.-5 P.M.

New Jersey

✓ ATLANTIC CITY

Louis Tussaud's English Wax Museum, 1235 Boardwalk, Atlantic City, N.J. 08401 (tel.: 609-348-0266). Hours: May-Sept.—9 A.M.-1 A.M. Closed rest of year.

New York

LAKE GEORGE

House of Frankenstein, 213 Canada Street, Lake George, N.Y. 12845 (tel.: 518-668-3377). (Located in downtown Lake George.) Hours: summer—9 A.M. to midnight. Shorter hours after the summer season until mid-Sept.

Waxlife USA, Box 511, Lake George, N.Y. 12845 (tel.: 518-668-2717). Hours: summer (through Sept. 7)—1 P.M.-11 P.M.; remainder of year—call museum for information.

NIAGARA FALLS

Niagara's Wax Museum, 333 Prospect Street, Niagara Falls, N.Y. 14303 (tel.: 716-285-3561). (Located opposite New York State parking lot.) Hours: 9 A.M.-11:30 P.M. through Dec. 1.

North Carolina

CHEROKEE

Wax Museum of Cherokee History, Cherokee, N.C. 28719 (tel.: 704-497-3081). (Located on U.S. 19 East.) Hours: open daily—Apr. 1 to Nov. 1; open at night—June 1 to Labor Day.

Ohio

ZANESVILLE

National Road Zane Grey Museum, Zanesville, Ohio (tel.: 614-872-3143). Hours: 9:30 A.M.-5 P.M. daily; Sundays and holidays—1 P.M.-5 P.M.

Oregon

NEWPORT

Royal Pacific Wax Museum, 550 S. West Coast Highway, Newport, Ore. 79365 (tel.: 503-265-2062). Check locally for hours.

Pennsylvania

GETTYSBURG

✓**Hall of Presidents and First Ladies,** Gettysburg, Pa. 23735 (tel.: 717-334-5717). (Located opposite Gettysburg Town Center.) Hours: summer—9 A.M.-10 P.M.; spring and fall—9 A.M.-5 P.M.

✓**National Civil War Wax Museum,** Steinwehr Avenue at Culp Street, Gettysburg, Pa. 23735 (tel.: 717-334-6245). Hours: Mar. 15 to June 1—9 A.M.-9 P.M.; June 1 to Labor Day—8 A.M.-10 P.M.; Labor Day to Nov. 1—9 A.M.-9 P.M.; Nov. 1 to Mar. 15—9 A.M.-6 P.M.

LANCASTER

National Wax Museum of Lancaster County Heritage, 2249 Lincoln Highway East, Lancaster, Pa. 17602 (tel.: 717-393-3679). (Located on Route 30, 4½ miles east of Lancaster.) Hours: open all year at 9 A.M. daily.

South Dakota

DEADWOOD

Ghosts of Deadwood Gulch Wax Museum, Lee and Sherman Streets, Deadwood, S.D. 57732 (tel.: 605-578-3583). (Located in the Old Town Hall.) Hours: June-Sept.—8 A.M.-6 P.M. Closed rest of year.

KEYSTONE

Shrine to Democracy Wax Museum, P.O. Box 132, Keystone, S.D. 57751 (tel.: 605-666-4455). (Located near Mt. Rushmore National Memorial.) Hours: daily June 15-Labor Day—8 A.M.-9 P.M.; May-June 14, after Labor Day-Sept. 30—9 A.M.-5 P.M. Closed rest of year.

RAPID CITY

Holy Shrine, Rapid City, S.D. 57701 (tel.: 605-342-8404). (Located on Highway 16 two miles south of Rapid City.) Hours: summer through Sept.—8 A.M.-6 P.M.

Tennessee

CHATTANOOGA

Hall of American Presidents Wax Museum, 3921 St. Elmo Avenue, Chattanooga, Tenn. 37409 (tel.: 615-821-4907). (Located next to Lookout Mountain Incline Railroad.) Hours: daily June-Labor Day—9 A.M.-9:30 P.M.; rest of Sept., daily, 10 A.M.-5 P.M.; Apr.-May, Oct.-Nov., Sat., Sun.—10 A.M.-5 P.M.; closed rest of year.

GATLINBURG

American Historical Wax Museum, 542-544 Parkway, Gatlinburg, Tenn. 37738 (tel.: 615-436-4462). Hours: June to Aug.—8 A.M.-11 P.M.; Apr., May, Sept., and Oct.—9 A.M.-10 P.M.; Nov. to Mar.—9 A.M.-5 P.M.

Christus Gardens, River Road, Gatlinburg, Tenn. 37738 (tel.: 615-436-5155). (Located one-half block from the center of Gatlinburg.) Hours: Apr. 1 to Oct. 31—8 A.M.-10 P.M.; remainder of year—Monday through Saturday, 9 A.M.-5 P.M.; Sunday, 1 P.M.-5 P.M.; closed first two weeks of Dec. and Dec. 25.

Dr. Gardner's Museum of Witchcraft & Magic, 600 Parkway, Gatlinburg, Tenn. 37738 (tel.: 615-436-5019). Hours: summer—9 A.M. to midnight; winter (Nov.-Mar.)—noon to 8 P.M.

Ripley's Believe It or Not! Museum, 800 Parkway, Gatlinburg, Tenn. 37738 (tel.: 615-436-5096). Hours: summer—9 A.M. to midnight; winter (Dec.-Mar.)—10 A.M.-6 P.M.

NASHVILLE

Country Music Wax Museum, 118 Sixteenth Avenue, Nashville, Tenn. 37219 (tel.: 615-256-8777). Hours: Sunday through Thursday— 9 A.M.-6 P.M.; Friday and Saturday—8:30 A.M.-8 P.M. (6 P.M. after Labor Day).

Texas

GRAND PRAIRIE

Southwestern Historical Wax Museum, 601 East Safari Parkway, Grand Prairie, Tex. 75050 (tel.: 214-263-2391). (Located off Dallas/Fort Worth Turnpike at Belt Line Road Exit.) Hours: Memorial Day to Labor Day—9 A.M.-9 P.M.; remainder of year—Monday through Friday, 10 A.M.-6 P.M., Saturday and Sunday to 7 P.M.

HOUSTON

Classic Car Showcase, 3009 South Post Oak Road, Houston, Tex. 77027 (tel.: 713-621-2281). Hours: May through Aug.—10 A.M.-6 P.M.; Sept. through Apr.—10 A.M.-5 P.M. Closed Jan. 1 and Dec. 25.

✓ SAN ANTONIO

Hall of Texas History, Lone Star Pavilion, Hemis Fair Plaza, San Antonio, Tex. 78205 (tel.: 512-225-2266). Hours: summer (May through Oct.)—10 A.M.-7 P.M.; winter (Nov. through Apr.)—10 A.M.-6 P.M.

Virginia

WILLIAMSBURG

Williamsburg National Wax Museum, Richmond Road, Route 60, Williamsburg, Va. 23185 (tel.: 804-229-8602). (Located on Route 60 at city limits.) Hours: June to Labor Day—9 A.M.-10 P.M., Mar. 15 through May and after Labor Day through Oct.—9 A.M.-9 P.M.; remainder of year—9 A.M.-5 P.M.

Washington

SEATTLE

Pioneer Square Wax Museum, 112 First Avenue, South, Seattle, Wash. 98104 (tel.: 206-MA4-6486). (Located in Pioneer Square.) Hours: summer (May through Sept.)—9:30 A.M.-10 P.M.; winter (Oct. through Apr.)—9:30 A.M.-5:30 P.M. Monday through Thursday, to 9 P.M. Friday, Saturday, and Sunday.

West Virginia

HARPERS FERRY

John Brown Wax Museum, High Street, Harpers Ferry, W .Va. 25425 (tel.: 304-535-6342). Hours: Apr. 1 to Dec. 1—9 A.M.-5 P.M.; Feb. and Mar.—open weekends 10 A.M.-5 P.M.; closed Dec. and Jan.

Wisconsin

WISCONSIN DELLS

Royal Wax Museum, 112 Broadway, P.O. Box 411, Wisconsin Dells, Wisc. 53965 (tel.: 608-254-2184). Hours: May to Sept. 30—9 A.M.-10 P.M.

Wyoming

JACKSON

Wax Museum of Old Wyoming, Box 1724, Jackson, Wy. 83001 (tel.: 307-733-3112). Hours: summer (May 1 to Sept. 30)—8 A.M.-10 P.M. Closed rest of year.

CANADA

Alberta

BANFF

Canadian Wax Gallery, 120 Banff Avenue, Banff, Alberta, Canada (tel.: 403-762-3501). (Located in Banff National Park.) Hours: early June through Labor Day—9 A.M.-10 P.M.; remainder of year—shorter hours, except Jan. 3 through Mar. 1 when gallery is closed.

British Columbia

VICTORIA

Classic Car Museum, 813 Douglas Street, Victoria, British Columbia, Canada (tel.: 604-382-7118). (Located behind Empress Hotel.) Hours: June 16 to Oct. 15—9 A.M.-10 P.M.; remainder of year—9 A.M.-5:30 P.M.

Royal London Wax Museum, 470 Belleville Street, Victoria, British Columbia, Canada (tel.: 604-388-4461). (Located at the inner harbor, opposite the Parliament buildings.) Hours: Easter to Thanksgiving Day—9 A.M.-10 P.M.; remainder of year—10 A.M.-5 P.M.

Ontario

NIAGARA FALLS

Biblical Wax Museum, 4921 Clifton Hill, Niagara Falls, Ontario, Canada (tel.: 416-358-3244). Hours: summer—8 A.M.-2 A.M.; winter—9 A.M.-10 P.M.

Boris Karloff Wax Museum, 6546 Buchanan Avenue, Niagara Falls, Ontario, Canada (tel.: 416-356-5220). (Located in Oakes Drive Motel.) Hours: June through Sept.—9 A.M.-11 P.M.; remainder of year—10 A.M.-6 P.M.

Burning Springs Wax Museum, 2760 Portage Road, Niagara Falls, Ontario, Canada (tel.: 416-356-1501). (Located at the Panasonic Centre.) Hours: daily July-Aug.—9 A.M. to midnight; May-June, Sept.—9 A.M.-11 P.M.; Oct.-Apr.—10 A.M.-10 P.M.

Houdini Magical Hall of Fame, 4983 Clifton Hill, Niagara Falls, Ontario, Canada (tel.: 416-356-4869). Hours: open daily 9 A.M. to midnight.

House of Frankenstein Wax Museum, 4973 Clifton Hill, Niagara Falls, Ontario, Canada (tel.: 416-356-8522). Hours: open daily 9 A.M.-1 A.M.

Louis Tussaud's English Wax Museum, 4915 Clifton Hill, Niagara Falls, Ontario, Canada (tel.: 416-354-7521). Hours: June to Sept.—9 A.M. to midnight; remainder of year—9 A.M.-9 P.M.

Movieland Wax Museum, 4950 Clifton Hill, Niagara Falls, Ontario, Canada (tel.: 416-358-3061). Hours: open daily 9 A.M. to midnight.

Pirate's Cove Wax Museum, 6671 Oakes Drive, Niagara Falls, Ontario, Canada (tel.: 416-356-7020). Hours: June through Sept.—9 A.M.-11 A.M.; remainder of year—10 A.M.-6 P.M.

Ripley's Believe It or Not! Museum, 4960 Clifton Hill, Niagara Falls, Ontario, Canada (tel.: 416-356-2238). Hours: June to Sept.—9 A.M. to midnight; remainder of year—9 A.M.-9 P.M.

Royal London Wax Museum, 5705 Falls Avenue, Niagara Falls, Ontario, Canada (tel.: 416-356-7488). Hours: June to Sept.—9 A.M. to midnight; remainder of year—9 A.M.-9 P.M.

TORONTO

Toronto Wax Museum, 385 Yonge Street, Toronto, Ontario, Canada (tel.: 416-863-1208). Hours: open daily 10 A.M.-1 A.M.

Prince Edward Island

CAVENDISH

Royal Atlantic Wax Museum, Cavendish, Prince Edward Island, Canada (tel.: 902-963-2350). (Located at the junction of Highways 6 and 13.) Hours: open May 15 to Oct. 15—9 A.M.-10 P.M.

Quebec

MONTREAL

Musée Historique Canadien Ltée., 3715 Queen Mary Road, Montreal, Quebec, Canada (tel.: 514-738-5959). (Located one block east of St. Joseph's Oratory.) Hours: May to Sept.—9 A.M.-9:30 P.M.; Oct. to April—9 A.M.-5:30 P.M.

QUEBEC

Musée Historique, Ltée., 22, rue Sainte-Anne, Quebec 4, Canada (tel.: 418-522-4245). Hours: June 1-Oct. 14—10 A.M.-10 P.M.; Oct. 15 to May 31—11:30 A.M.-5 P.M.; Monday through Friday and 10 A.M.-10 P.M. on Saturdays, Sundays, and holidays.

STE. ANNE DE BEAUPRÉ

Basilica Wax Museum (the Historical), Basilica of Ste. Anne, Province of Quebec, Canada (tel.: 418-827-3781). (Located near the Basilica parking lot.) Hours: Apr. 15 to Oct. 15—9 A.M.-4 P.M.

OTHER FOREIGN WAX MUSEUMS

(Hours should be checked locally.)

AUSTRALIA

Kings Cross Waxworks, The Village Centre, Kings Cross, Sydney, N.S.W. 2011, Australia.

FRANCE

Musée de Cire, 87, rue de la Grotte, 65100 Lourdes, France.

Musée Grevin, Boulevard Montmartre, Paris, France.

GREAT BRITAIN

England

Ripley's Believe It or Not! Museum, Central Promenade, Blackpool, England.

✓**Abbey Museum,** Westminister Abbey, London, England.

✓**Madame Tussaud's,** Marylebone Road, N.W. 1, London, England.

Jersey, Channel Islands

Elizabeth Castle Museum, **Jersey, Channel Islands.**

Mount Oriel Castle Museum, Jersey, Channel Islands.

Scotland

Edinburgh Wax Museum, New Assemblies Hall, 142 High Street, Edinburgh, Scotland. (This is one of the newest, most extensive wax museums in the world, featuring 150 costumed figures—designed by well-known theatrical designers—spread over four floors; it includes a section for young children.)

ICELAND

Reykjavik Wax Museum, Reykjavik, Iceland.

ISRAEL

Shalom Palace Wax Museum, Shalom Mayer Tower, 9 Ahad Haam Street, Tel-Aviv, Israel.

JAPAN

Kyoto International Wax Museum, 72 Building, Kyogoku, Kyoto, Japan. (This is now a traveling exhibit.)

Osaka Wax Museum, Namba Kagetsu Theater, Sennichi-Mai, Osaka, Japan.

Tokyo Tower Wax Museum, 4-2-8 Shiba-Koen, Minato-Ku, Tokyo, 105, Japan.

NETHERLANDS

Madame Tussaud in Amsterdam, Amsterdam, The Netherlands.

SPAIN

Museo de Cera Londres, Edificio España, Carretera de Cadiz 17, Torremolinos, Malaga, Spain.

INDEX